NORMAN MEIER

CREATE WEALTH

WITH

PRIVATE EQUITY AND PUBLIC COMPANIES

A guide for entrepreneurs and investors

authorHOUSE®

AuthorHouse™ LLC
1663 Liberty Drive
Bloomington, IN 47403
www.authorhouse.com
Phone: 1-800-839-8640

Published by AuthorHouse 04/10/2014

ISBN: 978-1-4918-7212-3 (sc)
ISBN: 978-1-4918-7263-5 (e)

Library of Congress Control Number: 2014904798

General disclaimer about my advice

Every bit of advice about making money, Private Equity, public companies, etc. is based on my personal experience and is not typical. You should consult a lawyer before you start any kind of money raising activity. I do not take any kind of responsibility for statements made. Any kind of statement may have errors, may not legally be viable, laws may have changed and the accuracy of my information might be false. The information cannot be used as proof in legal matters as some of the information might have been changed or altered to protect certain people involved. This information comes with the best intentions to educate and help other people.

The real secret of our economy: public companies

Have you ever wondered how people make
millions in the stock market?

Have you ever heard of someone who sold
their business for millions of dollars?

Do you want to know the real secret to business success in
the stock market by someone who has actually done it?

What I am about to teach you can normally not be found in a book. There are no business courses that you can take to obtain this knowledge or any other form of seminar that will teach you how to create wealth with a public company.

It is a secret that is very well protected by successful business people and professionals. It is a process that can make the difference between a small business trying to survive and a thriving business with financial strength.

What I am about to teach you is very specific knowledge that is literally worth millions of dollars. I will teach you how you can build a new company; get investors to finance it and to take it public in the stock market, where it will be valued at millions of dollars.

I will explain in detail how you can use Private Equity to get a company initially financed so that it has enough money in the bank to execute on its business plan and develop its business model.

The main goal of a Private Equity project is to build a company with substance and potential that can thrive in the public markets.

If you chose the right business model, get the company properly financed and take it public in the stock market, you can create a multi-million dollar company. If you own a majority share position in this company, it can change your life forever. The goal is not only to change your life but also to create happy investors.

Creating something substantial out of thin air

Think about the basic foundation of our economy. If you have an idea for a business, it is first merely a thought. You will take that thought or idea and manifest it into the real world. You will form a corporation, put in a business model, create the right share structure, finance the company, take it public in the stock market, get additional financing from institutional investors and finally create a multi-million dollar business.

Think about it. All the big companies in today's world were first a thought or an idea and then turned into big corporations that sell products or services and employ thousands of employees. The more time goes by the bigger and more valuable the company gets. And if you were the founder of this business with the majority of the shares in the company, not only will the company be worth millions but your personal net worth as well.

I will teach you several exciting business models that will be ideal for private equity and public companies. Resources deals like oil and gas, gold, silver are a great choice, for example, but also biotechnology and other new technologies. I will show you a typical company and how you can put together a similar deal without any previous knowledge about the industry.

I will show you how to find investors and build sales organizations that exclusively sell the shares of your company to raise capital for your projects. I owned several sales organizations during my career. One of them continually raised about one to two million dollars each month for about two years.

I will also show you how to finance real projects that make money using the money of the market place in a legal way.

As a former stockbroker in Europe and North America I can teach you everything about getting international investors and how to approach different markets.

In this program I will teach you the following things:

1. How you can **raise money** to grow your company and **go public**
2. How to **sell your stocks** in the market and **turn it into cash**
3. How to **find investors** that will buy stock in your company and give them a good return on their investment
4. How to build, structure and organize a new public company so that it can become **a $100 million company**
5. How to **market and promote the stock** of your public company so that many new investors will buy your stock
6. How to avoid common mistakes and pitfalls and stay 100% legal
7. How to turn **a business idea into a real company** that is publicly listed and **gets millions in institutional financing**
8. How to put together the right marketing material so that investors will buy your company's stock
9. How to **create a real exit strategy for your investors** so they make money and keep coming back to you for **new deals**
10. How to **choose a business model and industry** that will sustain good and bad times

Multi-millionaires and billionaires

How does someone become a multi-millionaire or even a billionaire? Well, it wasn't by working in a 9 to 5 job with a boss and a salary. And it wasn't by working two jobs or working overtime. Only 1% of people became rich because they can sing, act or won the lottery. Only 10% were doctors, lawyers or other professionals.

The answer is pretty simple. Over 74% were entrepreneurs. Nobody has done it by having a regular job or an income. The way that people become billionaires is by **owning a big share position** in a company.

If you really look at people like Bill Gates or other billionaires, you will find that there is really only one answer to this question. There is really only one way to become a billionaire. A person had an idea and built a business. The company eventually went public in the stock market and the company grew over time. The founders had a majority share position in the company and because of it they became billionaires. That is the only way it is possible unless they inherited it from a person who has done it just like that.

Let's make an example: Someone owns 10 million shares in a company and the stock price has gone to $100 per share—that's a billion.

Or someone has four major positions valued at $250 million each. He would have had to own 10 million shares in each deal and the company's share price went to $25 per share. I have seen deals like this many times.

Why not put yourself into a position that could allow that to happen?

Well not everybody is going to become a billionaire. And not everybody is going to be a millionaire—even though there are over 24.2 million millionaires in the United States alone today.

You can still have a public company and make money with it. You can use all this knowledge and make a nice income from operating the company. You decide how much your income will be by the size and efforts of your capital raising abilities and on how well you develop your company.

There are thousands of people who have done it before you and now enjoy the life they always wanted. You just need to know how it is done and then do the same things so that you will get the same results. If you follow through, your life will never be the same.

My story

How did I get involved in Private Equity and public companies?

Before I even started I got a job offer from UBS, one of the biggest banks in the world. They would have hired me to train their new employees in basic financial knowledge—a job that I could have enjoyed doing. HOWEVER . . .

My annual salary and bonus would have been $150,000. Not bad, you might think at first. But then I started to look into the future. If I needed $100,000 per year to live in Europe, then I would only have $50,000 left to save. In 10 years I would have $500,000 in savings. And that was the end of that job offer . . .

I wanted to become a millionaire no matter what it took. I wanted to be successful and I wanted to have recognition and make other people happy in the process.

In order to achieve these goals I needed to change my attitude, my character, my beliefs, my level of self-confidence, and my level of self-discipline. There was a point in my professional development where I was so broke that I couldn't pay my bills anymore. The obvious solution should have been to get a regular job. But I knew with a regular job, I would give up on my dreams of becoming a millionaire.

> I made the decision to try doing it no matter what and **rather to be homeless than to take on a regular job.**

Eventually, I discovered the power of Private Equity and public companies. I reached my goals in only two and a half years. But my career in the financial industry started long before that time.

When I was in my early 20s I became a financial planner. I started working for AWD, a European multi-level marketing company that sold financial products like mutual funds and insurance products to private clients. I worked there for six years and learned how to advise clients on how to improve their overall financial situation, increase the return on their investments, save taxes, life insurance, private insurances, mortgages and all other matters of financial planning. Even though we offered a great service to clients, we never advised them on individual stocks.

Then I went to Vancouver, Canada and became a stockbroker. Besides my basic education I also took many finance courses and got twelve different diplomas and designations in courses like portfolio management, derivatives (options and futures) and many others from the Canadian Securities Institute.

But all this education did not help me when it came to dealing with taking a private company public.

It started actually when I went back to Europe and after a short career in the hedge fund industry, I decided to become self-employed.

A friend of my father's needed some help. He had bought a public shell but it got delisted. Since I was a former stockbroker he asked me to help him to get it back onto the stock market. Since this guy was more of a businessman and sales person rather than a financial expert, he believed that I had the necessary knowledge to help him. Besides, he didn't speak any English and needed someone who could.

George, the person who hired me to help him turned out to be the biggest crook. He was running an illegal stock scheme and raised money from investors for his own pockets. Right at the beginning I realized how not to do it and always to stay 100% legally clean. George had some great talents and was not afraid of having a big vision, which was the one quality that I learned from him. But eventually he got arrested and I swore that I would do it better and legally.

Well, it was very exciting and I lost a few nights of good sleep but a long story short, I ended up getting the company listed again by simply flying back to North America, meeting with the securities lawyer, the accountant and the auditor. The stock got listed again and it was due to my efforts.

Then I began to think. Well, if I did this for someone else, why not do it for myself?

George was running an African gold deal that never turned into anything. I liked the idea of gold but I had no projects, no contacts and no geologists at that point in time.

I needed to make money and I wanted to do it the right way but I had no idea how to get started.

I knew that I wanted to have a US company. So I found a company on the Internet that did incorporations. I called them up and incorporated my first company. I had no idea about things like share structure or par value and I simply just chose some numbers that were standard. I also had no idea about the kind of business that I wanted to operate and therefore I chose my cat's name Hemis (actually Hemingway but his nickname was Hemis) to get started. I thought that I would change the name later once I would know what the company would actually do. But I never did change it. My cat's name turned into a $300 million company.

And here is where the magic of the Universe happened. Because I incorporated a company and gave it a name, an opportunity presented itself.

My wife's cousin had a friend who was working in the gold industry. She told me that he was a nice guy and great businessman and that I should simply meet him for a coffee to talk. And that is what I did. I told him about my plans and that I had no projects or geologists and I simply asked him if he could refer me to someone.

He gave me the name of a lawyer in Sonora, Mexico, showed me a Mexican gold project and gave me the contact information of a senior geologist from Utah who was working on that particular project.

I got a letter of intent (LOI) to acquire that project with the help of my friend and I used that project to get started with my new company.

I decided to fly to Mexico and met with the local lawyer and I looked at three gold exploration projects. I particularly liked one of the projects. It was called "El Tigre" and wanted to acquire it. When I sat down with the landowners, I had to negotiate the terms in my rusty Spanish and I ended up with the rights to the property. I am not sure if I did such a great job on the negotiation, but my Spanish teacher from school would have been proud of me.

Without any real knowledge about the industry I decided to take a courageous leap forward and just go with it.

The next step was to get money.

In the past, I only sold financial products from large and reputable companies. I could hide behind their name and size and it was easy selling them. But now I was faced with the most difficult kind of investment to be sold. I had to sell my plan, idea and myself without having any substance in the company whatsoever. I was selling shares of my own company, which in reality was basically just a piece of paper (the stock certificate), the ownership in my company. This was selling in its purest forms.

I put together a power point presentation and I made a list of all my personal contacts. I wrote a 2 page letter explaining what my new plan was all about and I sent it out to 50 people. Then I started calling everybody on my list and setting up personal meetings.

I also joined forces with my 50-year-old friend Bruno. Bruno was what we call a fallen angel. He used to be a rising star working for UBS, one of the biggest banks in the world, but after he had left and tried to start his own currency fund, it failed and he was over $300,000 in debt.

Since I was only 30 years old at the time and needed some credibility, I made him my CFO. He had a lot of contacts in the financial world in Switzerland and I had the ability to sell.

The first client that we got invested $5500. He bought 10,000 shares at $0.55, a price that we had decided to do our first round of financing.
The next one bought 20,000 shares for $11,000 and that was the result for our first month. So we had raised $16,500, which we used to form the Mexican subsidiary, pay for new marketing material and the rest we used for salaries because we were both broke.

Our business partnership worked well because we had clearly defined the roles we each held in the company. Bruno was a great door opener and because of his kind nature, people liked and trusted him.

Here is where Michael Gerber's book "The E-Myth Revisited" taught me a great lesson in advance. And the lesson goes like this: partnerships don't work out. That is very true because sooner or later one person feels like they are doing more than the other and should therefore be compensated better. The only exception to this rule exists if there are clearly defined roles and only one boss (not two).

We operated out of a room in the attic that was probably no more than 150 square feet. We always went to see the clients in their offices because our office was not very impressive at the time.

The next month we didn't get any investors and I got scared and depressed. I feared that I had dug myself into a hole and that I had to quit and pay back those two investors one day. I probably would have quit if it hadn't been for Bruno. He was full of enthusiasm and one particular day he told me about a couple of leads that he believed would invest about $50,000. His light-heartedness gave me new strength, and because of this I continued. He was right. Eventually, we were able to attract several more investors and even one who invested over $160,000.

This gave us momentum and opened up new options. Two days after we had received that money we flew to Mexico and started to look at two more projects that we wanted to acquire. In the end, we were able to secure 3 projects in Mexico and our money raising activities started to excel.

Before we knew it, we attracted several new investors and raised about one million dollars from about 20 more individuals.

Initially, our marketing material was very poor but because of our enthusiasm we were able to convince investors to invest into our deal. As time went on, we continued to improve our materials and things started to become more and more professional. In my opinion it is better to start with about 80% perfect than never to get off the ground with 100% perfect material and conditions. Especially in the beginning you need momentum. That is key.

As I was talking to more and more people I started to attract other sales people from other sales organizations. One person, who was involved with a church group, raised over $500,000 in one week for us. Another guy, who I ended up putting at the top of my sales organization, raised $250,000 in the first month.

I took three people who came from a different sales organization and I rented an exclusive office in the middle of Zurich. Within 2 to 3 months, we hired a total of about 25 new sales people who all started to sell my deal. This operation grew really fast and we started to raise about $500,000 to $1.5 million every single month. We raised $10 million in the first year alone.

With all the new money, I was able to get a lot of projects and geologists on board. I had continued the going public process with my lawyer and after 9 months, the SEC declared our filing effective.

More and more people joined our efforts to raise money and my organization grew. In the end, I had about 10 geologists, 10 admin people and the rest of my total 60 employees were mostly sales people. My operation became really big in a very short period of time and everything I set out to do, I achieved.

> Start small and finish big.
> That is what I learned from the founder
> of Subway when I read his book.

After the SEC declared the company's filing as effective, we filed our form 15c2-11 with the market maker and received our ticker symbol three months later. Before we started to trade, I did a 2 for 1 reverse stock split, which doubled the amount of shares and cut the price in half. People who bought the shares at $0.55 in the first round, now effectively paid $0.27 and the first price at which we started to trade was at $0.80 per share. It was a huge success and the price even went as high as $3.50 per share for some time but most investors sold their shares anywhere between $1.00 and $1.50. In the first year alone we had a volume of over 50 million shares. Not to shabby for project with a cat's name, don't you think?

When I decided to take the second deal public, it took the SEC only 16 days compared to the 9 months previously to declare our company effective. We were raising money at $0.50 per share and I got the company listed at $1.25 and the price went up to $2.00 within a few days.

Everything was great. I had taken two companies public and each one of them was trading successfully. We had raised over $40 million in about two and a half years and I had become a cash millionaire and a multi millionaire in stocks.

The best thing was that everything was 100% legal and I only had the best intentions to continue to grow and improve our companies. At the time I just turned 32 and I felt like the king of the world.

But soon I would be faced with the hardest challenges of my life so far. Looking back, I realized the mistakes that I had made. But at the time I felt like I made mostly the right decisions and if I had not trusted some people and giving away control, the companies might still be a success today.

Eventually, things started to fall apart. The stock prices started to drop. First with Hemis, then with Tecton. If there are more sellers than new buyers in the market, it will put pressure on the stock price and the price will drop—no matter how good your company and its potential is. I had hired a promoter to help with the marketing of the stocks and to create more volume. For that purpose I gave him free trading shares hoping that he would work in the best interest of the company and even that he would sell some to make some additional profits for me personally. But none of that happened. I lost big time. This promoter and his group had only their own interests in mind and started to sell off all their shares to turn them into cash for themselves. This put so much pressure on the stock prices that both of them fell down to a few cents eventually.

Well, it is during the hard times when lessons are learned. I also realized that even though I was not responsible for others greed and deceptions, that I still was in charge of the company and my poor judgment of people and making a couple of bad decisions of my own lead to my fall from grace. People called me a fraud and a cheater even though I only had the best intentions and I never did anything illegal. The worst was not the money that I lost but the loss of those who felt I had deceived them and the loss of my reputation.

In fact, it took me several years to recover emotionally from these events.

But this is not how my story ends.

Back then, my lawyer told me that all great dealmakers in the business had to go through a similar experience first before they became great again. The trick was to survive through this and come out stronger and more experienced on the other side. And this is exactly what happened. Today, I can look back realize what went right and what went wrong. Some things will never, ever happen again and I have put together some lessons for you that I learned from being in this business so that you hopefully don't make the same mistakes and can reach all your dreams and goals, without the heartache.

I ended up doing several other successful deals and got back on the horse. Ever since I have been involved with many companies as a director or consultant and I have continued my journey in the business of Private Equity and public companies.

In my first three years I raised over $40 million and what I built attracted over 500 investors. I have spent over $1.4 million in legal fees for my filings and IPOs. My first public company was valued at over $300 million in the stock market. As the main shareholder I personally owned $123 million of it. My second deal also went over $150 million in value and I owned about $40 million of it.

My monthly income was over $100,000 and I had everything that my heart desired. My personal cash position was $1.3 million and my newly built house was $1.5 million worth. I drove a Porsche Cayenne and my luxurious apartment overlooking the city of Zurich was $10,000 per month in rent.

Not every deal ended up working out and stayed at that level but I was making lots of money and working on a level of wealth that most people can only dream of.
I got a salary of $10,000 from 5 different companies and I got a few small percentages of the money raising activities, which ended up being about $50,000 per month.

In my whole career I raised over $400 million from private investors for all kinds of financial products and over $600 million from institutional clients. I have been a financial professional since 1995 and became an entrepreneur in the process.

When I was younger I so badly wanted to become a millionaire and a successful business owner but simply didn't know how to do it. I had read all the books about success from Anthony Robbins and Brian Tracy, got all motivated but I still didn't have a clear strategy on how to go about my goals. It took me years of reading, studying, listening to tapes and going to seminars until I finally figured it out.
I would have loved to have a mentor or coach who could have taught me this business but I didn't have anyone. Just like me,

there are thousands of people out there in the world who want to become successful and make money but who have no idea HOW to do it. I feel for them because I once was one of them myself.

I believe in the universal law of cause and effect from the Universe. I know that by teaching others to live better and happier lives, my own life will get better, too. I always wanted to be a success teacher for others. By writing this program, I am fulfilling my own dream and destiny.

Don't be intimidated

Even if you don't have a financial background or education, you can learn everything about this topic. The most important thing is that you understand the basics and the roadmap of how to take a company public. But you don't have to do it all by yourself. In any case, you will need to hire a securities lawyer and some other professionals to help you with this process.

You can compare it to driving a car: You should be able to understand the basic traffic rules and know how to drive a car but you don't need to build the car yourself and understand how the engine works. Initially, you will have a driving instructor and as time goes on you will be able to drive the car by yourself. Of course, you should continue to educate yourself.

The main thing is that you understand the importance of getting money into your company. Your job is to build or run the company.

Basics about Private Equity

Getting started

The main goal of this chapter is to teach you the basics of the business of Private Equity and public companies without going into every single detail. The main focus will lie on making a successful business venture happen combined with some basic technical knowledge without boring you with unnecessary details that will be handled by your lawyer or accountant.

I want to give you hope and a new opportunity to make your dreams happen and to show you how it can be done. I hope you will enjoy this exciting new information and that I can help you to become successful with your business.

You will get information about the following topics:

1. Introduction to Private Equity
2. Going public roadmap
3. Private placement offerings and financing options in a nutshell
4. Share structures and valuations
5. Product knowledge cases and business models
6. Sending out documentation and creating new clients
7. Business development
8. Conduct and ethics
9. Transfer Agent, share certificates and electronic shares
10. Trading stocks
11. Promotion and Marketing
12. Filings and SEC rules
13. Financial success with Private Equity
14. Most common terms
15. General business information

What is Private Equity and how does it work?

In simple terms: when a company is listed on a stock exchange, it is considered to be a public company. When it is not listed, it is called a private company. The term "Equity" simply refers to stocks or capital.

> Private Equity can be defined as investments in companies that are not yet publicly traded on a stock exchange.

An investor invests into a company that is still private (not traded). Through private equity a company can receive the necessary financing to advance its projects and to be successful. The idea behind such an investment is to either be able to sell the stocks in the market when the company goes public or that the company will be bought by a larger company and the investor will get his capital back that way. The investors are willing to purchase shares of this company at a relatively low starting price.

The company now intends to obtain a listing at a stock exchange or another similar institution, which will allow the investors to sell their stocks at a higher price than they originally paid for and thereby make a profit. The Initial Public Offering (IPO) will help them to get a so-called "Exit-Strategy" for their investment.

This "Exit-Strategy" is a very essential part of the whole private equity investment. Without such a strategy the company will have a hard time finding investors willing to support the company with an equity holding. This is the reason why one of the main goals or milestones of such a company is to make an IPO.

Private Equity as an asset class

Private Equity can be defined as an asset class consisting of equity investments in companies that are not yet publicly traded on a stock exchange. The purpose of private equity is to find investors who provide the financial resources to establish a start-up company that has to finance one or more projects. The investors are willing to purchase shares of this company at a relatively low starting price.

This exit-strategy is a very essential part of the whole private equity investment. Without such a strategy the company will have a hard time to find investors willing to support the company with an equity holding. This is the reason why one of the main goals of such a company is to make an IPO. But it's a long way until a company has reached the public listing at a stock exchange and it is not certain that the company will reach this step. Because of this fact, private equity investments are generally considered to be high-risk investments. In case of a successful IPO of the company the profits of such an investment can be enormous and way above average.

The definition of a stock

Plain and simple, a stock is a share in the ownership of a company. Stocks represent a claim in the company's assets and earnings. As you acquire more stock, your ownership stake in the company becomes greater. Whether you say shares, equity, or stock, it all means the same thing. Typically, for one common share you have one vote. The more shares you own the more control or influence you have in the company.

Being an Owner

Holding a company's stock means that you are one of the many owners (shareholders) of a company and, as such, you have a claim to everything the company owns in relation to your percentage ownership interest. As an owner you are entitled to your share of the company's earnings as well as any voting rights attached to the stock.

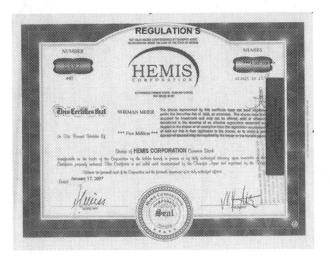

A stock can be issued as a share certificate. This is a fancy piece of paper that is proof of your ownership. In today's computer age, you won't actually get to see this document because your brokerage keeps these records electronically, which is also known as holding shares "in street name". This is done to make the shares easier to trade. In the past, when a person wanted to sell his or her shares, that person physically took the certificates down to the brokerage house or bank. Now, trading with a click of the mouse or a phone call makes life easier for everybody.

Being a shareholder of a public company does not mean you have a say in the day-to-day running of the business. Instead, one vote per share to elect the board of directors at annual meetings is the extent to which you have a say in the company. For instance, being a Microsoft shareholder doesn't mean you can call up Bill Gates and tell him how you think the company should be run. In the same line of thinking, being a shareholder of Anheuser Busch doesn't mean you can walk into the factory and grab a free case of Bud Light!

The management of the company is supposed to increase the value of the firm for shareholders. If this doesn't happen, the shareholders can vote to have the management removed, at least in theory. In reality, individual investors like you and I don't own enough shares to have a material influence over the company. It's typically large institutional investors and major shareholders who make the decisions.

For ordinary shareholders, not being able to manage the company isn't such a big deal. After all, the idea is that you don't want to have to work to make money, right? The importance of being a shareholder is that you are entitled to a portion of the company's profits and have a claim on assets. Profits are sometimes paid out in the form of dividends. The more shares you own, the larger the portion of the profits you get. Your claim on assets is only relevant if a company goes bankrupt. In case of liquidation, you'll receive what's left after all the creditors have been paid.

Another extremely important feature of stock is its limited liability, which means that, as an owner of a stock, you are not personally liable if the company is not able to pay its debts. Other companies such as partnerships are set up so that if the partnership goes bankrupt the creditors can come after the partners personally and sell off their house, car, furniture, etc. Owning stock means that, no matter what, the maximum value you can lose is the value of your investment. Even if a company of which you are a shareholder goes bankrupt, you can never lose your personal assets.

Debt vs. Equity

Why does a company issue shares? Why would the founders share the profits with thousands of people when they could keep profits to themselves? The reason is that at some point every company needs to raise money. To do this, companies can either borrow it from somebody or raise it by selling part of the company, which is known as issuing stock. A company can borrow by taking a loan from a bank or by issuing bonds. Both methods fit under the umbrella of debt financing.

On the other hand, issuing stock is called equity financing. Issuing stock is advantageous for the company because it does not require the company to pay back the money or make interest payments along the way. All that the shareholders get in return for their money is the hope that the shares will someday be worth more than what they paid for them.

It is important that you understand the distinction between a company financing through debt and financing through equity. When you buy a debt investment such as a bond, you are guaranteed the return of your money (the principal) along with promised interest payments. This isn't the case with an equity investment. By becoming an owner, you assume the risk of the company not being successful—just as a small business owner isn't guaranteed a return, neither is a shareholder. As an owner, your claim on assets is less than that of creditors. This means that if a company goes bankrupt and liquidates, you, as a shareholder, don't get any money until the banks and bondholders have been paid out; we call this absolute priority. Shareholders earn a lot if a company is successful, but they also stand to lose their entire investment if the company isn't successful.

General risk assessment

This is what the financial planning pyramid looks like:

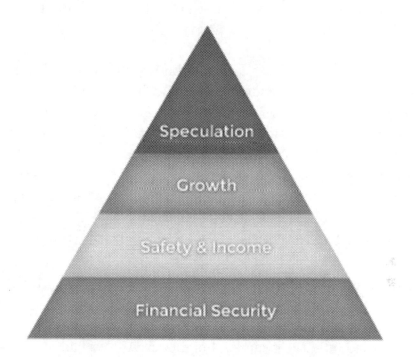

Of course this is just a rule of thumb. A detailed analysis of assets should always take place before a possible purchase of shares or any other investment.

On risk, there are two important rules:

- There is basically no investment without risk.
- The higher the possible return, the higher the risk.

> "There is nothing that happens without a risk, but without taking risks nothing happens at all."
> Walter Scheel, former German president

Expectations of the investors

It undoubtedly is the desire of every single investor to get the highest possible return on his investment and minimize the risk to almost zero.

An experienced investor certainly knows that he won't find a possibility, which provides a maximum return with having a minimum of risk at the same time. There is simply no investment available that has risk, return and a short investment horizon perfectly matched. The only thing you can do to achieve a good balance between risk and return in your investments is to combine potentials by putting together a diversified portfolio.

Great growth expectations

Imagine you had the chance to buy shares from Coca Cola or McDonald's BEFORE they were officially listed on a stock market. A very small amount of money would have grown a thousand fold and turned into a large amount of money. All you had to do was to wait for the company to go public and expand its business.

It is easy to look back in time and to use those examples. But there are more opportunities available today than ever before. There are thousands of new start-up companies with a promising product that need funding. Up to recent years, these types of investments were only available to institutional clients and big investors. Private Equity has been made available to everybody these days and it is an asset class that can produce great returns. The Internet and growing new technologies have made it possible for new companies to get attention like never before.

The variety of Private Equity investments

Private Equity is the term for venture capital of not publicly traded companies, which comes from private and institutional investors. Such an investment can be made in many different development stages of a company; e.g. for the financing of an expansion, a management-buyout, a turnaround, a transition period or the beginning of a new business venture.

Each stage of a company opens up a whole range of different chances and risks. Provided that there is an existing business idea with great potential for success and an experienced management, which is working on the development of the young company, chances for success are great.

The pre-IPO stock purchase

The very basis of a young company consists of a promising business idea and a product that has a good potential for success. To secure the financial support for the development of the company, there is a need for investments from private investors. For this purpose, the company offers shares to potential investors. The price of the shares depends on the development stage of the company.
Supported by these investments, the company will reach a certain stage that justifies presenting it to the free market.

The private investors have thus given the company a sound financial basis to develop its business and initiate the IPO. From the IPO, the company receives additional financial means to pay for the company's development. The IPO also allows the pre-market investors to sell their shares on the free market or to store them, like any other capital asset, in their personal portfolio. If the shares are bought pre-IPO the company will issue a share certificate. This certificate then can be put into a brokerage or trading account. If the shares are not traded yet then there will be no price available in the system yet. As soon as the company is public, a price will be visible.

The advantages of private equity

- Not exposed to the fluctuations in stock market
- Being part of a project from the beginning
- Relatively low starting price
- Above average growth potential

The decisive factors for success

- The idea must stand out from the crowd
- Market potential for the product must be provided
- Management is key
- Initial Public Offering and trading volume for exit
- Adequate funding must be available
- Price-to-earnings ratio (P/E ratio)
- Attractive price and share structure

Turn an idea into reality

One of the most rewarding things is to create something out of thin air that will later become a company. An idea or a thought for a business will be described in a business plan and investors can buy shares of the company. The company uses a blank share certificates and will print the names of investors on it.

Investors who believe in an idea will buy shares and receive a share certificate in return. Basically, it is just a piece of paper in the beginning and it is something that doesn't cost the company anything.

Now with the money that the company has received from investors the management will try to make the business work.

Even though most new businesses are a risky venture, you never have to bear the whole risk alone. The risk lies mainly with the investors who put up the money. Initially, to get started, you will also have to put up some of your own money into the venture but once things are off the ground the business can be financed with outside capital from investors. The main goal is to make things work and you will try to do your best to make the business work.

This is how the business world works. People are willing to put money into a venture because they believe that their investment will be worth more in the future. As long as you inform them of the risks involved and they are still willing to invest their money, then you are fine. Start-up companies are always very risky and because things are still uncertain und unstable, the risk is much higher but so is the potential return.

The interesting thing is that a lot more people are willing to risk their money than I originally thought. Greed is so dominant in our society that it becomes stronger than reason. People also hope to have a lucky punch and make money overnight with one good investment. Interestingly, this kind of thinking is existent in a lot of people.

Everybody has heard of someone who bought a stock and it went through the roof. And people would also like to be part of something like that.

Take a look at the people around you

If you take a look at the richest people in the world, you will find out that they have one thing in common. Not one of them had a job. They owned companies that went public in the stock market, expanded and got valued at millions or billions of dollars. And that is the answer. You will only become very rich if you decide to have a business that becomes big.

In my opinion, the greatest invention of all time was to be able to form a company. Think about it. Someone has an idea, incorporates a company, hires people, sells products and makes a profit. It provides hundreds of people with an income for themselves and their families. It starts to have a life of its own. If you do it well enough, and often enough, it will expand and grow.

Eventually, you can take the company public in the stock market. You will get millions of dollars in extra financing for your business so you can expand it even more and make more profit. As the owner you can pay yourself a salary, a bonus, dividends, get more shares, loan money against your shares and so on. The possibilities to make money are endless.

Microsoft Corporation

Microsoft went public on March 13, 1986. If you were able to participate in the initial public offering and buy 1000 shares at $21 for $21,000, your shares would be worth over $7 million today. The stock has split nine times since the beginning.

> What if you had shares of Microsoft **BEFORE**
> it was offered to the public?

You might have $14 million instead of $7 million or who knows? Maybe even more.
That is the attractiveness for investors to buy private shares of companies before they are listed. If you have a good story, you

will get the money from investors to finance your business and therefore your dream.

Getting the Money You Need to Finance Your Business

If you are starting your own business you will need money. Depending on your business idea you might not have the necessary funds to realize your idea.

Most people think that they need to get a loan from a bank to get started. They soon realize that banks are not willing to lend money without any collateral. Very often this marks the end of most business dreams.

Another way to finance your business idea is to get money from private investors. We have seen a lot of people with great business ideas struggle to get money from investors. The problem was often that they either had no clear strategy on how someone could invest into their business, that the investor would take over too much of the business or that there was no clear exit strategy for the investor to be motivated enough to invest in the first place.

The solution is Private Equity. A business should be set up from the start in such a manner that there is a structure and plan for investors to be able to buy shares of the company. There needs to be a clear share structure in place so that the owner of the business does not lose control but at the same time allows investors to participate.

Financing a company through private placements

Typically a person with a good idea for a product is trying to build a business and make it successful. Unfortunately, over 85%

of all start-up companies close down in the first three years due to lack of capital.

Another reason for business failure is the inexperience of business knowledge and the absence of an effective sales and marketing strategy.

In order to help a new company grow and become successful, you need to raise capital through private placements. A private placement is an offer to buy shares from a company that is still private (not yet listed on a stock exchange).

Before a company goes public it is possible to have several private placement financing rounds to raise capital for the company. A company could offer shares in the first round at $0.30 and later in a second offering at $0.40 before it goes public at $0.50. Depending on the business and industry, the company can raise several million dollars to further grow and develop its business.

The most important thing for investors is to have an exit strategy. Once a company is publicly traded, an investor can sell his shares in the market.

A private placement offering typically has an attractive price per share and the investor is hoping to be able to sell his shares when they are public at a higher price.

PRIVATE EQUITY FINANCING PROCESS

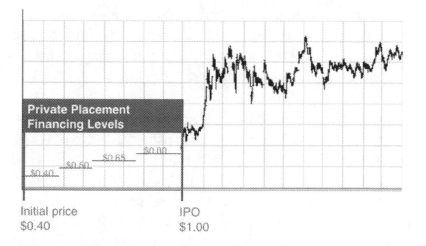

When looking at a stock chart, it is only possible to see the first price when the company was first listed. The company however has been around for a longer period of time and usually got financed through private financing rounds. These financing rounds are called private placements. If a company does a first round of financing at, for example, $0.40 a share, it might raise capital for future business development. The company might continue to raise capital by using several financing rounds before it goes public. These rounds may be at the $0.50, $0.65 or the $0.80 level. The general public will then only be able to buy stocks when the company is listed at $1.00, for example. But investors who were able to buy the stocks for $0.40 per share have already more than doubled their money.

The advantages of Private Equity investors are that there are no price fluctuations, are able to participate in the beginning of a new venture when the price of a share is at its cheapest, have a high return on investment potential and a relatively short investment horizon of only 6 to 24 months.

If you are selling shares to accredited (wealthy) private investors of companies that are not yet listed or trading, the transaction is called Private Placement and is an offer to purchase shares of private companies. The plan is to finance companies that will eventually go public in a stock market. By doing so you are offering your investors attractive investment possibilities with a chance of getting high returns.

As a director of the company you are legally permitted to sell shares of your own company to private investors in the US. The SEC differentiates between two types of investors: accredited investors and non-accredited investors. Accredited investors are people who either have $200,000 in personal annual income or $300,000 in household income or have $1 million in net worth excluding the equity in their home. Because your company is new and bears more risk than an established company, the SEC has limited the number of non-accredited investors to 35 people. There is however no limit to the number of accredited investors.

As a director of the company you can either sell shares on your own or get the help of a broker dealer who can help you with selling the shares to investors. If you can convince a stockbroker who is licensed with a Series 7 and is working for a broker dealer, he or she can help you to finance your company much faster because he usually already has established client relationships.

In order to raise capital, you need to write a prospectus about your company. This prospectus is called a PPM (Private Placement Memorandum). A PPM is a document that describes every single detail about your company and has an offer to raise capital in it. It is also called a legal prospectus. For example, it could say in your offering that you would like to raise $5 million by issuing 10 million shares at $0.50 per share in a specific time frame (mostly 2-3 months).

> The specific knowledge that you can obtain by understanding Private Equity is worth millions of dollars. This knowledge will enable someone to create new companies and to create value in the stock market beyond a normal scope.

Using Private Equity, investors are able to participate in the beginning of a new venture when the price of a share is at its lowest. Just as it would have been a good opportunity to own shares of Microsoft before it went public, you can offer shares of a promising new company. The investor is involved at the beginning of a new venture with a high return potential. Usually, the investment horizon is relatively short—anywhere from a few months to three years.

The main motivation for someone to buy a new start-up company lies in the potential gain.

> A big company like McDonald's is unlikely to double in price within one year. But a small start-up company can double, triple or go up ten times.

Private Equity example

Let me give you an example: The founding members of the business have issued 20 million shares in total. They have decided to sell an additional 10 million shares to private investors for $0.50 per share. This means that the company would get $5 million into its bank account. This money can be used to develop the business, pay salaries and be used for other business related things.

> The investor needs to have a motivation to invest into a company. But more importantly, he needs to know when he can expect to get his investment back.

Therefore you need to plan an IPO for your company. Assuming that you are able to list your shares with an initial price of $1.00 per share your investors would double their money. This will give them the necessary motivation to invest in the first place. Your job is to build the business and create revenues. A typical time frame for the investment can be anywhere from one to three years. During that time you need to develop your business in such a way that the number of shares multiplied by the share price will be equal to the value of the company in the market.

Private Equity—Raising money for your own business

You should create a company in such a way that investors are willing to participate in your company by buying shares and giving you money for it. I have encountered a lot of people who had great business ideas but they had no clear strategy on how to structure a way for people to invest. They either had to give away too much of the company for a relatively small amount because they were desperate to get any money at all or there was no clear exit strategy for investors to get their money back some time in the future so that it was not a motivating concept. Because of the lack of structure and exit plans most people will never get money from private investors.

A person only wants to invest into a project if there are clear rules and there is a short-term time frame of two or three years in which the investor will get his initial investment plus profit back.

In only two and a half years I was able to raise over $40 million from private investors for my projects.

People were able to buy shares at $0.55 in the first round, $0.70 in the second round, $0.90 in the third round and $1.20 in the final round. The shares got listed at $1.60 and everybody was happy. People were able to sell their shares through their brokers in the market and they made a good deal with this investment.

You could structure your company in such a way that you issue 10 million shares for yourself and sell another 10 million shares at different levels to investors. If you go public you will have issued a total of 20 million shares and if your share price is at $1.00 per share your company will be worth $20 million in the market. If you were able to raise capital at an average price of $0.50 per share you will have raised $5 million for your company. With this money your goal is then to expand your company and do your best to increase the value of your share price.

> Once your company is public you are able to get money from institutional investors and investment houses. This will open up a whole new world of financing options.

What you need in the beginning is a securities lawyer who can set up the structure for you and an accountant who will make sure that everything is in order so that the SEC (Securities and Exchange Commission) will approve the filing (also called S-1 registration statement) of your company.

The lawyer will prepare an offering memorandum (prospectus) and a share subscription agreement (a contract to buy shares from the company) to that you have the necessary tools to sell shares.

All you need next is a corporate account for people to invest their money into.

Taking your company public

There are a number of substantial advantages in having a public company. It is a possibility to raise a lot of capital and therefore expand the business. It gives the company new financing options and it provides an exit strategy for the founders.

Typically, a financial institution that acts as an underwriter leads a going public process. This financial institution takes the company through the entire going public process and also gives a commitment for a multi-million dollar financing.

However, this process is only possible for medium to larger companies that are already well established.

But there is also a solution for start-up companies. A securities lawyer can do the necessary filings with the SEC (Securities and Exchange Commission). The company has to provide audited financial statements and if everything has been approved, a market maker will file the form 15c2-11 with the NASD to obtain a trading symbol.

Even though there is no initial multi-million dollar financing attached to it, it opens up a whole new world of opportunities for financing options because the company is publicly traded.

The cost for taking a company public for start-up companies can vary. It is somewhere between $50,000 to $250,000 depending on the scale of the business, the extent of the audit, time needed with the lawyer and other factors. If you have set up your business the right way so that investors can buy shares of the company while you wait for your listing, you should easily be able to raise the necessary funds to pay for all the professional fees involved.

Also, once you are trading you can sell shares in the market to generate cash for the business. If you have the right people working on a marketing strategy for your stock, you should be able to create enough trading volume to turn some of your shares into cash.

There are a number of ways to get your company listed. You can do it in the USA or in Europe. I prefer the NASDAQ OTC BB (Over-the-counter bulletin board) and the Frankfurt Exchange. Those are good places to get started. For resource or mining companies I suggest a listing in Canada.

You can either incorporate your own company preferably in the state of Nevada due to a lot of good reasons or you can buy an existing company that is already listed but is no longer a working business. This is called a shell. You buy the shell that is listed and trading in the market and you merge it with your existing business. You can change the name of the listed company to your company's name and you restructure with the help of a securities lawyer the share structure. Within a very short period of time you have a public company. This is also called a reverse take-over or reverse merger.

Incorporating in Nevada

Why should you choose Nevada? Well you should know some of the history and development of Nevada. Today Nevada is one of the fastest growing states in America and Las Vegas is the fastest growing city in America.

Every year 40,000 new jobs are created by a new hotel and 60,000 people move there each year. There are more and more technology companies in Nevada and because of its tax advantages it becomes increasingly more attractive to new industries. However, this was not always the case . . .

In the year 1859, when gold was first discovered near Virginia City, Nevada was mainly controlled by people who lived in California. During the gold rush mainly the region of San Francisco profited from this development and for more than 60 years rich people from California controlled Nevada. Nevada was more like a colony and the governors and senators made sure that the interests of the people in California were taken care of. Even today, 80% of the land in Nevada is owned by people in California. Because of this, the corporate law in Nevada became very flexible and was in serving the purpose and interests of Californians.

Here are the main advantages:

1. Taxes: Companies pay no state tax. Some companies save millions because they were incorporated in Nevada.
2. Flexibility: Directors, officers or shareholders don't have to live in Nevada, nor do they have to have their annual meetings there. Even foreigners (non-US persons) can be directors. One director can hold all positions in the management at the same time and you don't even have to be a shareholder in order to be a director. You can even hold your meetings on the other side of the world by telephone and you can change the bylaws of the company in such a way to give you the most flexibility possible. This kind of flexibility and freedom makes it extremely attractive to have a Nevada company.
3. No minimum capital: You don't need to put money into the company in order to incorporate it.

4. Annual fees: The annual filing fees are $125 plus $200 per year for the business license.
5. Privacy: Officers and directors can stay anonymous and appoint a "nominee director". This is a person who will appear in the official filing so that the real directors can stay anonymous. This will however have to be disclosed once you are a public company. But as long as your company is private, no one will ever know who is behind the company.

What about Delaware? Delaware also has a lot of advantages but it is more advantageous for companies who make millions of dollars in revenue. If you intend to stay at a normal level, you will be better off with a Nevada company.

Incorporating a US company

Incorporating a US company is very easy. You can use a service company who will do it for you or you can do it yourself by filing with the secretary of state. The cost is typically a few hundred dollars. You will need a registered agent to accept any legal documents or documents from the secretary of state.
There are also lots of services like mail forwarding, telephone number, fax number, etc. that you can get to make your business appear to be a local company.

In order to open up a bank account you will need a TAX ID or EIN (Employer Identification Number). You can get this from the IRS website or from the service company that incorporated your company. Typically, you will have to be present in person to open up an account.

In order to issue share certificates you can issue them yourself by buying a hundred blank certificates and print the names of the investors onto it or you can sign up with a transfer agent who will do it for you professionally. Both ways are legal but if you intend to raise lots of money and want to go public, I would urge you to pick a transfer agent. It is way more professional.

When you incorporate a company you will need to define the amount of shares authorized and the par value. The minimum par value in Nevada is $0.0001. This is just a theoretical value and nothing to do with the actual stock value. But when you first incorporate a company, there is no value. In order to acquire shares you will have to put money into the corporate account. So the lower your par value is, the less money you will have to put into the account to acquire for example 10 million shares.

You can have common shares or preferred shares or both. I used to only have common shares because it made things a lot less complicated. But today I feel that you should have for example 80 million common shares which are intended for the investors and which each have one voting right and 20 million shares should be for the founders and the management team. You can assign a 10x voting right to the preferred shares so that you will not lose control over the company so easily. Also, you can assign a special dividend right for the preferred shareholders in case you need to take out some money. All this can be defined in the bylaws of the company when you incorporate.

You will have to have a minute book of your corporation. The minutes are basically nothing else but a summary of a meeting where some decisions were made for the company. You can also make a corporate resolution to officially make a decision and have it filed on paper. This is always necessary for important decisions for the company.

Once you decide to build a share structure there are a number of questions that you should ask yourself right from the start. You basically will need to plan your company and its share structure backwards. So ask yourself how your company will ideally look like if it is fully financed and then go back and define the steps.

Here are some important questions for you:

- Which strategic share positions should you already issue right from the start so that you will have the necessary shares later? (If you issue 1 million shares at $0.00001 for marketing services it is much better than to declare them later if your financing round is at $0.50 per share and you will have to justify a $500,000 expense on your books.)
- How much money do you want to raise in each financing round?
- What is your end goal in regards to money raising for the next 12 months?
- At what exact price levels should you be raising the funds so that you don't issue too many shares? (The goal is to keep the amount of shares that are issued low)
- If you intend to list your company at $1.00 per share and you have 50 million shares issued, you will have a market capitalization of $50 million. Is that going to be justified in relation to the projects and money that you have acquired? Will there still be enough additional potential in the stock price later?
- Should you issue more shares at $0.00001 in the beginning as a strategic position to keep control and to have enough shares for promotion, marketing or other services available? (You can always cancel shares later)
- Should you issue shares for the transfer agent, accountant or other professionals?
- What share structure will make most sense if you are going to promote your deal in the future?

Possible price strategy

1. Financing round: $0.0001 (Founding members)
2. Financing round: $0.001 (Strategic partners for promotion)

3. Financing round: $0.01 (Intermediaries, Transfer Agent, etc.)
4. Financing round: $0.10 (Friends and family round, certain investors)
5. Financing round: $0.25 (first round for investors)
6. Financing round: $0.50 (second round for investors)
7. Financing round: $0.75 (third round for investors)
8. First price at listing: $1.00

From incorporating to money raising

1. Incorporation
2. Select management team
3. Open up the bank account (EIN, 2 different IDs, articles of incorporation, initial list of officers)
4. Organize share structure and pay initial amounts into the account (to acquire shares for the management team members)
5. Develop business plan
6. Acquire first project ($10,000—$50,000)
7. Hire corporate securities lawyer ($5000 retainer)
8. Hire corporate accountant ($3000 retainer)
9. Create marketing material
10. Create PPM—Private Placement Memorandum
11. Create SSA—share subscription agreement
12. File Form D with SEC (Securities and Exchange Commission)
13. Set up company with a transfer agent to issue shares
14. Set up administration (office address, telephone, email, hire assistant part-time, computers, etc.)
15. Start selling shares (raising money for first round of financing)

Securities law, lawyers and filings

In order to properly raise capital and not to break any laws, you will need to get a securities lawyer. This is not just any kind of lawyer but a specialized lawyer who deals with the SEC, EDGAR filings and knows about public companies.

As long as your company is still private you really have a lot of freedom and flexibility on how you run your company. There is no requirement to open up your books. But as soon as you go public, everything will need to be disclosed and there are a lot of rules that you must follow to be compliant with US securities law. Therefore, you need to start following certain rules while you are still private if you intend to go public later. The way you acquire your shares, how you start raising money or how your company is set up are all crucial factors that can make you or break you later. The most important thing will be your financial statement and how you do your transactions. Your financials will need to be audited and you cannot afford to make any mistakes.

Typically, you will need to file a S-1 registration statement (legal prospectus and disclosure document) with the SEC, file your 10-Qs (quarterly financial statements) and 8-Ks (material change).

Share structures

In order to raise money from investors you need to have a clear plan in advance. You should put together a share structure of how many shares will be sold to investors and how many shares will stay in the hands of the founders.

A basic plan could look like this:

	Shares issued	Price / par value	Capital raised
Founders	20 million shares	$0.0001	$2000
1st round	5 million shares	$0.10	$500,000
2nd round	5 million shares	$0.20	$1 million
3rd round	5 million shares	$0.50	$2.5 million
First price when trading		$1.00	

In this plan you will raise a total of $4 million and $2000. The $2000 is the first amount of money that the founders have put into the company themselves. The more money you put in yourself the better it looks for some investors. They want to know that you also put in some money and that your own money is also at risk.

The par value is the assigned value when you incorporate the company. It doesn't really say or mean much. It is the price level when there is nothing in the company so far.

Once you add value to the company you can raise the price to the next level. To add value you could acquire a product, assets, get a new management member, an option to buy a project or some other event that justifies an increase in the share price. When you are doing private placements there is no hard rule to calculate the share price. It is an estimate that the management team makes to increase the share price to the next level.

Structure your company

There is no right or wrong way to structure a share structure of a company. However, there are a lot of factors that need to be considered right in the beginning when you are setting up the initial share structure to avoid problems later or to keep work and cost down.

Typically, when you incorporate a company you will authorize 100 million shares. This should be enough for the start so that you have enough shares available to get started. The number of authorized shares can always be increased later by having the majority of the shareholders to vote in favor of increasing the number of authorized shares. Authorized shares are not issued shares and therefore this is only the number that is the maximum allowable amount of shares to be issued.

There are common shares and preferred shares. Common shares are typical for normal investors and they each have one vote. Preferred shares have special rights like extra dividend rights, extra voting rights and other features. Ideally, I would structure a company in such way that the management team and founders have preferred shares and investors have common shares.

Total authorized shares: 100 million
Preferred shares authorized: 20 million
Common shares authorized: 80 million

In the company's bylaws at the time of incorporation you should define that the preferred shares have 10x the voting rights over common shares. This way you ensure that you will never lose control when you issue more shares to investors.

Let's say that you only had one vote of the preferred shares and the same for common shares. If you issued 20 million for yourself and 20 million for investors, you will be dependent on investors to vote in favor of your future changes and to get reelected at the annual general meeting to be CEO or president again. Therefore, you want to keep control over the majority of what is going on in your company for as long as possible.

Transfer Agent, share certificates and electronic shares

Public companies typically use transfer agents to keep track of the individuals and entities that own their stocks and bonds. Most transfer agents are trust companies. Transfer agents perform three main functions:

1. Issue and cancel certificates to reflect changes in ownership. For example, when a company declares a stock dividend or stock split, the transfer agent issues new shares. Transfer agents keep records of who owns a company's stocks and bonds and how those stocks and bonds are held, whether by the owner in certificate form, by the company in book-entry form, or by the investor's brokerage firm in street name. They also keep records of how many shares or bonds each investor owns.
2. Act as an intermediary for the company. A transfer agent may also serve as the company's paying agent to pay out interest, cash and stock dividends, or other distributions to stock—and bondholders. In addition, transfer agents act as proxy agent (sending out proxy materials), exchange agent (exchanging a company's stock or bonds in a merger), tender agent (tendering shares in a tender offer), and mailing agent (mailing the company's quarterly, annual, and other reports).
3. Handle lost, destroyed, or stolen certificates. Transfer agents help shareholders and bondholders when a stock or bond certificate has been lost, destroyed, or stolen.

Stock certificates

The physical piece of paper represents ownership in a company. Stocks are the foundation of nearly every portfolio and they have historically outperformed most other investments over the long run.

Before online brokers and personally directed accounts, holding a physical stock certificate was a necessity, as this was the only way to authenticate stock ownership. This is not the case anymore. Although you may not need to hold a stock certificate, you may request one. The corporation you are holding stock in issues stock certificates, and you can get your certificate either directly from the issuing corporation, or by contacting your broker who may get the stock certificate on your behalf.

Detailed on the stock certificate itself will be your name, the company's name and the number of shares you own. There also will be a seal of authenticity, a signature from someone with assigning authority authenticating the certificate and either a CUSIP or CINS number. Currently, stock certificates are seen more as collectibles and souvenirs than actual records of ownership.

Issuing shares and sending them to clients

Step 1:
A client signs an SSA (Share Subscription Agreement)

Step 2:
The SSA goes to the company.

Step 3:
The management of company will issue (write) a corporate resolution (written decision or action of the company) where the management decides to issue new shares.

Step 4:
The directors of the company sign the corporate resolution and send it to the Transfer Agent.

Step 5:

The Transfer Agent will issue (print) new shares. If the shares are restricted, then the shares have a red stamp (legend) on the certificate. If the shares are free trading, then there is no red stamp.

Step 6:

The shares will be sent to the company. The company will then send the shares to the client.

Step 7:

The company will send a confirmation letter to the client of the share purchase.

Documents needed:

- Signed SSA
- Check or wire transfer (paid into the account of the company or of an escrow account with a lawyer)
- Proof of payment (Either a copy of the check or a confirmation of the wire transfer)
- Copy of the client's ID
- CIF (Client Information Form)

Rule 144 (red stamp = selling restriction)

The Hemis certificate has a red stamp from the Transfer Agent and it means that it is a restricted share certificate. The Tecton certificate has no red stamp and therefore is free-trading.

Turning a physical restricted share certificate into free-trading electronically traded shares

When you have a restricted share certificate, you will need to send it to the Transfer Agent after the restriction period is over along with the following documents:

1. Instructions to issue a new certificate that is free-trading
2. Pay the fee of about $20 per certificate
3. A legal opinion (a letter from a lawyer confirming that the shares are now free-trading according to the law)

The Transfer Agent will then issue a new share certificate without any restrictions. This new certificate can then be given to the broker or bank and will be put into the account. The clearing firm of the broker will then turn the physical shares into electronically traded shares.

Sending out documentation and creating new clients

A typical way to raise money is to send some marketing material about the company to potential investors. I would recommend sending out a 2-pager with a basic overview about the company. Too much information can sometimes confuse investors and lead to more questions and objections.

It is crucial that your company's marketing material and website are flawless and professional. You are selling a start-up company that has little substance and only a lot of plans and potential.

In the US you have to legally send out the PPM (Private Placement Memorandum) with your marketing material. Just keep in mind that the material itself will never ever convince a client to invest. It is only the sales person or consultant who can make that happen. The PPM is an anti-selling brochure. It describes all the risks and everything that could go wrong. Therefore you should focus on the relationship with the client and not on the material because it can scare away investors.

Putting together the right marketing material so that investors will buy your company's shares

This is what you should have:

- 2 pager (Corporate overview and key facts)
- Power Point Presentation as a PDF
- Website
- Corporate brochure
- PPM (Private Placement Memorandum)
- SSA (Share Subscription Agreement)

Of course you could have additional things like a third party report, an independent report, videos, pictures, etc. but in the end a person will only invest because of another person and not because of the marketing material. However, the marketing material must be perfect and cannot have any mistakes or look sloppy.

In my opinion it is always best if the president or founder creates the material because he knows best what is in the company and how to represent it.

Private placement offerings and financing options in a nutshell

When a private company is looking for capital it can offer a private placement financing round. A private placement is a private offer to sell shares of the company. It is supported via a private placement memorandum (short PPM), which is a legal document that describes and discloses every detail about the company. It is also called a legal prospectus.

The offering contains the number of shares, the time length of the offering and the amount of money to be raised.

Example:
10 million shares (amount of shares to be sold), $5 million (amount to be raised), $0.50 per share (price level) and starting January 1st until February 15th (6 weeks time frame).

There are several ways to do the offering:

1. Best efforts basis
2. All or nothing
3. Mini-max

If the goal of the company is to raise $5 million but they only raise $500,000 in the 6-week time frame, with the best effort basis, they can close the offering and accept the $500,000 even though it was not the desired amount. They can also extend the time frame for another few weeks if they desire to do so. I usually prefer this type of offering because it gives the company the most amount of flexibility.

The money will either go directly to the corporate account or an account that was opened by a lawyer on behalf of the company and the offering.

If there is an all or nothing type of offering and only, for example, $2.5 million of the desired $5 million was raised in the given time period, then the $2.5 million will go back to the investors, no commissions can be paid out and the offering will be canceled. I would not advise to do this kind of offering because $2.5 million is still a good amount and all the people who did all the work of finding investors will not get paid their commission. This type of offering is only good for investors who want to make sure that the company raised sufficient funds for a particular project.

Offerings can also be over-subscribed. Even though the company intended to raise only $5 million, it is possible that they were able to raise $8 million in this time period. In that case they can either increase the offering after the fact and accept the extra $3 million or they do the first come first serve principle and only accept $5 million at $0.50 per share. They could immediately do a second offering at $0.80 for the remaining $3 million and see if the investors would accept the new terms.

A mini-max offering will say that the company needs to raise a minimum amount of money, like $1 million for example, and the maximum amount that they will accept is going to be $7 million at this price level.

There is also the option of a unit offering. A unit is comprised of one common share at $0.50 and half a warrant for example. A warrant is an option to buy more shares, basically a right to buy more shares, at $0.65 per share and good for 2 years for example. This type of offering makes it a bit more attractive in case the stock goes beyond $0.65 in the future.

<u>Successful companies</u>

Let me give you some **real life examples** of companies that were successful in the market but started out as a small business first:

1. Greystar Resources went from $0.70 to $13.00 per share.
2. Energy Metals went from $0.25 in the first round of financing to $6.25 in less than two years.
3. Alumina Copper was offered as a private placement and the company was later sold for over $425 million.
4. Hemis was initially offered at $0.27 per share and the share price rose to over $3.50.
5. Tecton did a private placement at $0.50 per share and the stock quadrupled to over $2.00 per share.
6. Linear Gold went from $1.80 to $9.00 in less than 12 months.
7. Arc Energy developed from $6 to $20 in 6 years.
8. Cumberland went from $0.50 to $9.50 in 7 ½ years.
9. El Dorado was offered at $1.00 and rose to $10.50 in 4 ½ years.
10. Halo Resources was initially offered at $0.10 per share, got listed at $0.50 and went to $1.50. 1500% increase!

The list could go on and on of other successful deals that started small and turned into great deals.

There are many other business people who have used the road to go public and made lots of money with their companies. And what others have done before you, you can do as well.

Regulation D, S and Form D

Typically, an intended listing in the US with US investors is a Regulation D Rule 506 offering. Regulation S refers to a filing with the SEC if you only have foreign or non-US investors.

Before you start your money raising efforts you need to file a Form D with the SEC via EDGAR to make your intentions known. You can hire a service company or a lawyer who can do this filing for you.

Making money before the company is public—Earning examples of Private Equity

Private Equity is a way to sell shares of your company and in return people will put money into the corporate account. If you do your job well, you will be able to raise several hundred thousand or a few million dollars. This money is intended for the operations of the company, of course. However, there is no company if there are no people who operate it. So if you are the president of this company, you can pay yourself a salary. You can decide yourself what this salary should be. As a director of a company you can also pay yourself a bonus or issue additional shares as compensation.

As long as you do things that are reasonable and don't hurt the company, you should get paid for the work that you put in. Everybody understands and agrees with this.

There are a few ways to earn money:

- Salary: You can pay yourself a monthly salary. Example: $5,000 to $10,000 a month. For a CEO of a company that is very reasonable and on the low end.
- Bonus: You can have a plan and if the business reaches a certain milestone or goal, you will get a bonus: Example: $20,000
- Consulting services: Instead of being part of the company as management, you could work as an external consultant.
- Expenses: If you need to travel a lot, you can charge your expenses to the company. These could be things like air travel, your car, your phone, hotels, etc. If you are actively traveling and doing things this could easily be a few thousand dollars a month.
- You sell a portion of your own share position to new investors. You could for example sell 200,000 shares for

$0.50 that you originally paid $0.0001 for. This would give you an additional $100,000.

- Depending on your business, you could acquire a piece of land privately or through one of your companies and then sell it for a higher price to the company. The difference would be your profit.
- You can plan on selling a nice portion of your share position once your company goes public. You could for example sell 500,000 shares for $1 per share in the first month of going public.

(Before doing any of the above things please discuss with your lawyer.)

These are some great opportunities to make money before the company is public as long as you keep the best interests of the company and your investors at heart. Keep also in mind that if you can make your investors happy with the first deal, almost all of them will invest what they did before and more into your second deal.

How to create personal wealth with a listed company

If you personally own 10 million shares of your company and your company goes public at $1.00 per share, then your personal wealth is $10 million. If you can sell your share position in the market and turn it into cash, then you have it made.

So the plan is to build a company, sell shares to investors and raise money for the company, go public and then sell some of your shares in the stock market.

Basics about Public Companies

Reasons for investing into a company before it goes public

Before the company goes public it will do several private placement financing rounds for private investors. After the IPO, the price will be driven by supply and demand. In any case, the price will be higher than at the beginning. Investing into a pre-IPO stock is an exciting adventure, especially if you have a stock that will go through the roof. Every investor who owned shares in Microsoft before the company was public became a millionaire. Just like any new company, Microsoft started on the NASDAQ OTC BB.

Even though big companies have a lot more money and people than new start-up companies, smaller companies have much more growth potential than larger companies. The main reason is that big companies have already established projects already included in its stock valuation. If you want to profit from big gains, you need to get into a stock before it announces the next big discovery.

A company can have the best products or services, but if the investing public does not know about it, the stock will not be successful. Therefore, it is important to have a plan to create volume and market attention for when the company begins trading.

Our company has developed a clear plan with finance professionals to create an exit for the initial investors.

Going public roadmap

There are two ways to get your company listed. First, you can file a registration statement with the SEC and go through a process that will take about six to twelve months to complete. Secondly, you can buy a listed shell and do a listing by doing a reverse merger.

In order for a company to go public, it needs to fulfill four criteria.

1. The company needs file an S-1 Registration Statement with the SEC (Securities and Exchange Commission). A registration statement is a 50 to 60-page document that describes everything about the company. It explains the company's products, its risks, the share structure, the financials, etc. It is a disclosure document that shows all the facts about the company.
2. The company needs to have audited financial statements. The corporate accountant will prepare the financials of the company but an auditor will have to check them and declare them as audited. The audited financial statements will be part of the S-1 for the SEC.
3. The company will need to have at least 35 shareholders to go public. This number is a minimum guideline and is necessary so that a "market" of several participants can be justified.
4. A business model or product. The SEC will not judge your business idea nor will it approve it. It will simply have to be explained and all the facts need to be disclosed.

Once the company's lawyer has filed the S-1 registration statement, which is also considered a prospectus in the legal lingo, the SEC has 60 days to respond. It usually comes back with questions to clarify some points. Those questions are called comments. The goal of the SEC is to cover all the aspects of disclosure of the company so that every investor is aware of the potential risks when investing into a company. The SEC will not approve or disapprove of anything. All they want is to have disclosure.

The corporate securities lawyer will then respond to those comments and file an amendment to the original S-1. The SEC might come back several times with new comments but eventually; they will declare the S-1 as "effective". This means that the company provided sufficient information and facts.

The next step is to file a form 15c2-11 with FINRA (Financial Regulatory Authority). If the SEC is the lawmaker, then FINRA is the enforcer or financial police if you like. In order to do that a company will need to find a market maker who is a member of FINRA. Only a FINRA member firm can sponsor a company to get a symbol and to get listed. The market maker will file this form on behalf of the company and it is basically the same information provided in the S-1 but with the main focus on the share structure and the amount of free-trading shares. FINRA is the result of a merger between the NASD (National Association of Securities Dealers) and the NYSE (New York Stock Exchange).

The reason why FINRA will check the share structure and the amount of free-trading shares is to ensure that there is an actual market for the shares. If only a few people were shareholders, then they would decide what the share price would be and it would not be considered a fair market. They will also check whether the 35 shareholders are actual people and that is why each investor will need to provide an ID as well as a proof of their payment from their own account.

Otherwise one could just create 35 fake people and pay 35 times $100 in the company to create the minimum shareholder base. But in reality it would still only be the original owners who would control the company and its share price.

We could also incorporate 35 different companies and make them the shareholders. But FINRA will also check that factor because they will need to know each "control person" behind each corporation who is a shareholder. If they find out that it is again a couple of people, then they will not approve the filing.

Another rule that they will check is that the 10 biggest shareholders cannot control 90% or more of the free-trading shares. In that case, they would also come to the conclusion that it is not a fair market.

Anyway, after FINRA has reviewed the 15c2-11 filing (or short "the form 2-11") they can also come back with several comments until they are satisfied. But once they are satisfied, they will assign a trading symbol or ticker symbol to the company.

In the filing, the market maker has to submit a trading range for an opening price. Let's say that the company did several private placement financing rounds at $0.50, $0.70 and at $0.90, then it could submit a range of $1.00 to $1.20 for example. It should be near the last private placement. Typically, the market maker and the company decide on the first price range.

Once the symbol has been assigned, one of the shareholders, who has free-trading shares will put in a sell order into an online brokerage account. This order will be received by the market maker as the first order and only order and then he can fill it. That is the very first trade and now a price will be published in the system. The market maker has 30 days exclusiveness in this stock. After that period is up, other market makers are allowed to come in.

In the beginning only the people involved with the company know the ticker symbol. It is a four-digit letter symbol like ABCD for example. Unless it is a very big and known company, the IPO is a very quiet event. No one really knows that you are public now and there is almost no trading activity in your stock. If you want to change that, you will have to make it known with promotion and stock marketing.

Listing via Reverse Mergers

A reverse merger is basically a reverse takeover. A reverse merger is the acquisition of a private company by a public company to bypass the lengthy process of going public. In most cases there is a shell corporation (a corporation without an ongoing business which is listed on a stock exchange) who takes over a company, which isn't publicly listed yet. A significant disadvantage is the high price of several hundred thousand US-dollars for such a shell corporation.

Institutional financing

The biggest challenge is always to get money in the beginning to get your company off the ground. The first couple of million dollars are usually the hardest to get. However, if you offer shares of your company in a Private Placement transaction to private investors and you make the right connections, you should be able to raise the money.

Once you are public and have a proven business model, you can get institutional financing from mutual funds, investment banks or other financial institutions. Typically, at that point you will need cash to expand your business and to be able to grow. Getting $20 million as a loan or an investment in your company is very realistic if you have done a good job initially. It is actually easier to get $20 million than to get $2 million.

Institutions look for proof of management and proof of concept. If your business model works and can be expanded, the doors for millions of dollars for your company are wide open.

Reading and understanding a listed stock profile

Fancy Corporation

Authorized shares	100 million shares
Issued and outstanding	20 million shares
Free trading	12 million shares
Restricted shares	8 million shares
Fully diluted	22 million shares
Share price	$1.50
Volume	100,000 shares
Market cap.	$30 million
Working capital	$1 million
Warrants outstanding	2 million shares

When a company has 100 million authorized shares it means that it can issue up to 100 million shares but only the ones that are issued and outstanding are important for now. In order to calculate the value of the company or the market capitalization you multiply the issued and outstanding shares with the share price.

Warrants are nothing else but options that have not yet been exercised. And working capital refers to the amount of money that the company has in its bank account.

One of the most important factors is the volume. The volume will show you how actively traded the company is and how much it is in demand at the moment.

Technical Analysis—understanding charts

Technical analysis refers to chart analysis. There are a number of indicators like volume or moving average for example that describe the development of a stock. Learn everything you can about charts. It can be a great help to understanding a stock.

Fundamental Analysis—company numbers

Fundamental analysis refers to things like earnings, earnings per share, P/E ratio, revenue, EBIT (earnings before interest and taxes) and cash.

These are all underlying factors or financial indicators that show the strength of a company. Often, a company can have great fundamentals but the stock price doesn't reflect it. In that case, a company would be undervalued.

Valuations and market capitalization

There are two basic valuation formulas:

Formula 1:
Amount of shares outstanding x share price = market capitalization

Formula 2:
Annual earnings x P/E ratio (price per earnings) = fair valuation

Explanation

Assuming a company has issued 50 million shares and a current share price of $4.00 per share, and then the market capitalization is $200 million. (See formula 1)

This calculation is not based on the success of the company or any other factor but is solely based on math. The share price might be too high or too low based on the operations of the company but if the market is willing to pay $4.00 for a stock, then that is what the price is and therefore the market capitalization or value of the company is.

In order to get an idea whether the valuation is fair, we need to apply the second formula. Let's assume that the company is having earnings of $20 million per year and if you multiply this number with the P/E ratio, you will get a fair valuation of what the company should be worth.

The P/E ratio is a number that varies from industry to industry. It is simply a factor of many years of earnings a person would be willing to pay to buy the whole company.

Let's look at an example: Assuming you were interested in buying a business that generates $1 million per year in earnings. How much would you be willing to pay for it? If you were willing to pay $5 million for it, you would have amortized your investment in 5 years. The P/E ratio is the factor 5 or 5 years.

When it comes to private companies being bought, the P/E is anywhere from 3 to 5 but when it comes to listed companies, the average P/E ratio is 15. With more conservative businesses or old economy industries it is around 10 and with more dynamic industries it is around 25.

If we now consider that the annual earnings of $20 million are being multiplied by 10, then a fair valuation would be $200 million. In order to get the share price you need to divide the $200 million with the amount of shares outstanding (the shares that the company has issued) which is 50 million in our example and therefore the share price is $4.00.

Based on these simple calculations you will get a guideline of whether a company is over or undervalued in relation to its annual earnings.

Of course other factors can also be important for the valuation. Some things are intangible and cannot be taken into consideration with a formula. These might be factors like ability to increase earnings, stability of the company, market position, etc.

This also means that a company can be valued higher because of its positive outlook even if the current numbers are not reflecting it. If someone is convinced of the long-term potential of the company, investors or the market is willing to pay a higher price today.

Earning predictions for the next few years

The following are an example for earning predictions and the stock valuation. But the numbers will show what could be possible if the company can reach all its goals.

Product	Price	Amount per day	Earnings per month	Earnings per year
Oil	$100	250 bbl per day	$750,000	$9.0 million
Natural gas	$3	1500 mcs per day	$135,000	$1.6 million
Annual earnings				**$10.6 million**

Possible valuation and calculation of the share price

Calculation and valuation of a fair share price:

1. Annual earnings of $10.6 million x P/E ratio of 15 = $159 million market capitalization / valuation

2. $159 million: 50 million shares outstanding = **$3.18 per share**

Dilution of the share structure

In order to have a solid share price later when you are public, you should make sure that you don't issue too many shares unnecessarily.

If you have, for example, 300 million shares issued and a share price of $0.10 per share, you market valuation is $30 million. Instead you could have only 20 million shares issued and a price of $1.50, which will be much better because you will have more stability in your stock.

If you issue too many shares it will be hard to get a good valuation and to keep control. As a general rule you should remember that less shares is better than too many outstanding.

Usually it is companies that have something like 500 million shares outstanding and a share price of a few cents that will never recover. In that case you will have to do a reverse split and completely restructure your company.

Reverse split and restructuring your company

Sometimes it can happen that your share price has fallen to a few cents and it is difficult for you to get the share price back up. The only option that you will have then is to restructure and do a reverse split.

If you have, for example, 500 million shares outstanding and your share price is at $0.01 you could do a 250 to 1 reverse split. In that case you would end up with 20 million shares and your share price would jump up to $2.50. Now you have a better level to continue and you could then issue 10 million shares for an acquisition of a new project. Your ability to do a financing round at $2.50 is also better because you could do a PIPE financing (Private Investment into a Public Entity) at for example $1.80 with a 6-month holding period. This would enable you to raise additional capital for the company and to get things moving again. It would not be possible to get investors at $0.01 interested to do a financing.

OTC BB, NYSE, Pink Sheets, Frankfurt and other stock markets

Typically, you will start trading on the OTC BB. Once you qualify with certain standards (like market capitalization, earnings, volume, etc.) you can mature to a bigger stock exchange like NYSE AMEX (formerly known as American Stock Exchange), NASDAQ or you can even co-list in Frankfurt, for example.

One level below the NADAQ OTC Bulletin Board is the "Pink Sheets" stock exchange. It's an unregulated electronic stock exchange. The name "pink sheets" comes from the old shares, which were printed, on pink paper. Pink sheets are typical "Penny stocks" and very volatile. They can also be traded regularly but mostly; pink sheets are shares from so called "fallen angels"— companies that are on the ropes. But nevertheless there are some exceptions—companies with an ongoing business that are listed at the "pink sheets"—because since it does not require to satisfy any conditions to be listed at this stock exchange (no periodic financial statements, etc.), the companies can save up to $100,000 per year compared to a listing on other stock exchange

In summary, it can be said that there are many ways for a company to get listed at a stock exchange. But they all differ in the amount of time and money it needs to obtain this listing. Audited financial statement. This will increase the value of the company, which will now very soon be able to register for the OTCBB. The disadvantage: The high price of a shell corporation (for the RTO) of more than $100,000.

The other option is to start trading the "pink-sheet"-listed shares to once fulfill the requirements for the NYSE AMEX. To be listed there the company needs to have a minimum number of 800 shareholders and a trading volume of 500,000 over a certain period of time or either have a market cap of at least $75 million. The fees for an AMEX-listing are $65,000 for the first time, afterwards $25,000 per year.

Proof of concept and proof of management

Your goal must be to get the first one or two million from private investors to get your company up and running and to take it public. To organize the first million is the hardest task. Organizing $10 million or $20 million later on will be much easier.

You basically need to find people who are willing to give you money for your idea at a stage where the company is still very unstable und the risk is at its highest.

Either those people are greedy, inexperienced when it comes to investments or a bit naïve. You basically have to find those people who are willing to risk their capital (they are always out there) and to get from the starting point zero to level 1. Level 1 means that you are public and that your basic business model is operational.

I once had a long conversation with the head of the department of the energy and metals division of a large New York financing company. Randal, the head of that division, had over 200 analysts that were working for him and he was in the business of finding companies in the natural resources industry. He told me that it would be no problem to give me $25 million in financing for an oil project if I can prove two things:

1. Proof of concept
2. Proof of management

He was looking for a project that was already producing and proving that the business concept was working and being profitable. Therefore if the business concept or model is working and earning money then it can be duplicated somewhere else.

The second important part is proof of management. If the management had the ability to attract investors, get the project or product, take the company public and do everything else to bring it to the next level, then they have proven that they are capable of running this business and being able to duplicate the efforts all over again. That is also why it is typical if a group did a deal successfully the first time around, that they will get the funding immediately for the second project.

A management's ability and reputation is key. If they have done it before successfully, it is a good indication that they can do it again.

Those two factors are vital for funding success with institutional investors. If you can get the first couple of millions and develop the company from zero to a first level, then you have got it made. The next step will be that you can get financing from institutional investors.

The company has to be public for institutional investors to invest

Private investors will give you money if they believe in your story. They won't be able to sell their shares until the company publicly listed and trading. Institutional investors, like mutual funds, pension funds, banks, investment banks, etc. will not buy shares of a private company. The reasons are because they need to be able to sell their position into a liquid market if the stock loses value and that they need a valuation on their books for accounting reasons. A private company does not yet have a proper valuation and therefore would be listed as zero value in their books.

Therefore you will need a public vehicle to get institutional financing.

The process of getting money from an institutional investor is always the same. They will do a due diligence process. Basically, they want to know everything and see everything. You will have to provide financial statements, SEC filings; business plans, marketing material, etc.

An institutional investor wants to buy a deal that is undervalued and has growth potential. Therefore, they want to see if the company has the ability to increase sales and market share. The money that they will provide should solely be utilized to expand the business and therefore the valuation of the company and its share price.

An institutional investor is all about the numbers and not much about emotions. A $25 million financing is considered a small investment for an institutional investor and therefore if you ask for financing make sure to ask for a rather a larger sum of money and try to make a business plan that will show how this money can be used to fulfill this plan.

How to build, structure and organize a new public company so that it will become at least a $100 million company

The main goals have to be the following things:

1. Develop a business model that produces a profit or has a large potential
2. Attract the first couple of million from private investors
3. Have a share structure where you don't have to give away too much of your company in the beginning only because you need the money
4. Take your company public and get it listed.
5. Develop a proof of concept
6. Show that the management team has the ability to perform and that not too much money has been taken out or used for personal salaries
7. Show the ability to attract further projects for the company
8. Develop a plan that will show how institutional financing will turn this start-up company to grow into a $100 million business
9. Chose a product, market and industry that has less risk and prove how you can mitigate additional risks
10. Show your ability to have a big and clear vision and that your leadership is strong

Selling your own stocks in the market and turn them into millions

As soon as you get your symbol, you can make the first trade while you are coordinating it with the market maker to get the first quote (bid and ask). But at that point nobody really is aware that you are trading now. That's why you need to create some news and attention in your stock to create new buying volume.

The amount of shares that you have registered in your S-1 filing is the shares that are free trading. Everything else is still restricted.

Example: you have issued 20 million shares for your group and for your investors but you have only registered 8 million shares in your filing to control the float of the free trading shares in the market. The 8 million shares are 16 shareholders at 500,000 shares each. Those 16 shareholders are you and your management team and 10 companies that you have under control. Therefore, no one who is an outsider has really any free trading shares. It is only your inner circle that you control.

And that's how it has to be. You absolutely must have 100% control over the float (float = free trading shares). Otherwise you will have no control over the outcome of your share price and it is very likely that most people will sell off their position right away. The more people sell, the more pressure on the price and then the downward trend has begun.

If you intend to have a successful development of your share price you will need to have more buyers than sellers for the share price to go up. The only way you can do that is to limit the amount of free trading shares available to new buyers and to increase the demand for your shares. The more buying orders go into the system while only a small amount is available, the better for your stock.

Legally, 100% control is not possible. But everybody is doing it anyway otherwise you deal is doomed right from the start. You will have to set up 10 to 20 offshore companies and issue shares for them, which are less than 5% (4.9% ideally) of the total issued shares. This way you can register those shares in your S-1 filing and make them free trading.

The problem in the US is the amount of restricted stock versus the amount of free trading stock. You want to make sure that your investors will have restricted shares according to Rule 144 and give them an additional contractual holding period of 6 or 12 months once you are public. This is important because otherwise you will not be able to create a positive development on your price chart. Most people are sellers unfortunately and they want to make money as soon as they can. Therefore you must control every single position as much as you can. Only if you control most free trading shares can you make good money. The goal must be that you and your group are the only sellers with available shares for new buyers. The ultimate goal should be to sell something like 10, 20 or even 30 million shares into the open market that come from your position.

Making money after your company is public

Owning shares in public company

How do you get to own shares in a public company? You have to be one of the founders at the beginning. Example: If you form a new corporation and issue **5 million shares for you personally** and the company gets financed and goes public **at $1.00 per share**, then your personal net worth will be **$5 million.** Very simple.

> So the plan is to build a company, sell shares to investors and raise money for the company, take it public and then sell some of your own shares in the stock market to turn your share position into cash.

<u>Raising money for your company BEFORE and AFTER it is public</u>
If you have a good business model and the right legal vehicle to raise capital for your business, you can earn a commission for every dollar that you raise for the company.

Let's say that you are able to raise $10 million from 100 private investors in the course of 12 months. If you pay yourself a 10% commission on monies raised, you will have earned **$1 million!** This is called doing a private placement into a private company. But you can also do it AFTER the company is public. You can have your company listed first with almost no investors in the beginning. You start with the public shell and then you do what is called a PIPE financing: Private Investment into a Public Entity. It is exactly the same process of raising money and selling shares to investors but with the only difference that your company is already public.

<u>Brokering a deal between a company and a financial group</u>
Depending on the connections that you have you could earn **$1 million** simply by putting two parties together. Assuming that you have an agreement with a company who will pay you a 3% finder's fee for finding the right financial institution who will fund their company, you can make lots of money, too. All you have to do is to find the right two parties, make an agreement and bring them together.

<u>Selling your own share position</u>
Assuming you own 10 million shares in a company that you are about to finance through investors. You decide to keep 8 million shares and sell 2 million shares privately for a discount of 50%. If your company's stock is priced at $1.00 per share and you sell 2 million shares at $0.50 you will have made **$1 million** in cash. (Depending on your jurisdiction there are legal ramifications about the process but it can be done.)

Having a long-term stock position in a deal

You could start a company and issue 100 million shares to investors. You personally keep 10 million shares in the company that you decide not to sell right away. Assuming that your business will grow over time and become more valuable (with or without your involvement), it could eventually turn into a company that is worth $500 million in the stock market. By maintaining your 10 million shares you could end up with a net worth of **$50 million.**

Doing a promotional stock campaign

This can be the fast track to becoming rich. Once a company is listed on an exchange you can initiate a promotional program to make your stock more known. The goal is to create a lot of attention and volume in the stock so that a lot of new investors will buy the stock in the market. If you are the only person selling initially and you are offloading your entire share position, you could make millions in a very short period of time. I have seen many promoters that were able to sell 10 million shares over the course of 3 months into the market at an average price of $3 to $4 per share. By selling the entire 10 million shares into the market, they made over $30 to $40 million in as little as 3 months.

Once a company is listed on an exchange you can initiate a promotion program to make your stock more known. The goal is to create a lot of attention so that new investors will buy your stock via their broker. This will create a lot of volume in your title.

Without any new buyers your stock will not be actively traded and nothing happens. There is no point in having a public company if no one knows that it exists. There are over 13,000 listed companies in the US and you need to do something that brokers and investors will be attracted to your title.

There are a number of marketing strategies that you can use to create market awareness. Things like newsletters to potential investors, research reports or online presence in stock portals are just a few to mention.

The main goal of a promotional program is to sell your or the company's shares. Typically, a company hires a promoter that is the only person with free trading shares. The promoter has, for example, 10 million shares available and initiates a marketing program. Usually, he has a lot of contacts of potential buyers or lists of people that are interested in buying new issues. He puts the company in the best light possible and sends out marketing material to those potential buyers. The buyers get interested and put in orders through their brokers to buy your shares. Since you or the promoters are the only people who are sellers you sell your positions to new investors.

I have seen many promoters that were able to sell ten or even twenty million shares between $2 and $4 per share and make millions like that in a few months only.

The company releases news releases every week and by showing that the price of the stock keeps going up and up it is able to attract more and more investors.

Here are some examples of companies that had a high volume over a certain period of time with a reasonable price:

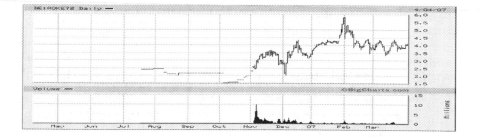

In the month of November there were over 20 million shares traded with an average price of $3 per share. That is $60 million!

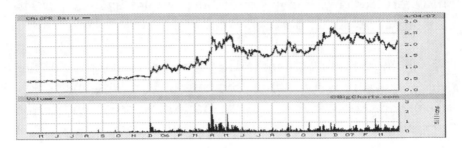

In April the average price was about $2 per share. I would say that at least 12 million shares were traded that month. A total of $24 million!

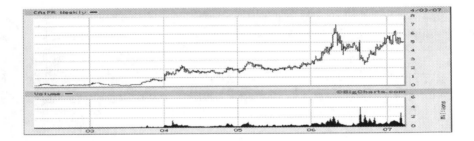

In the last year of this chart with an average price of $4 per share I would guess that at least 50 million shares were traded. That is over $200 million!

So if you are able to build a company, take it public and then be the only party that can sell, you can become very rich in a matter of days. If you are able to sell 10, 20 or 30 million shares in a few months between one and two dollars, then you are set for life!

Even if you are able to sell a few hundred thousand shares or a million in three months, this can make you a lot of money.

Depending on your stock marketing budget, the quality of your company and therefore the daily average trading volume, you should be able to sell at least anywhere from 2000 to 5000 shares per day without hurting the stock price.

Assuming that your average price per share is $1.00 that would result in $2000 to $5000 daily income. If you trade stocks on 20 days in a month, it could be up to $100,000 in one month.

One of the most successful and powerful German promoters was only 26 years old but he made at least $10 million per deal that he promoted. He never actually founded any companies but he learned how to promote the stock of a public company to attract new buyers. He signed up newsletter writers and developed strategies that would create a lot of new buying volume in a stock. In this program I will show you all the strategies that people like him are using.

Building public companies and selling the shells
In order to go public you can make the necessary filings with the SEC (Securities and Exchange Commission). You will need a company, a project, at least 35 shareholders, audited financial statements and a securities lawyer who will help you with the process. You might be looking at spending between $50,000 to $200,000 and it might take you 6 to 12 months to go public with your company.

But there is also a faster way to go public. It's called reverse merger. You can buy an existing publicly listed shell and merge your company into this shell. This way you are public right away and you don't have to wait 6 to 12 months. But to buy a shell like this you will need about $500,000.

The way you can get this money is through investors by selling them shares of your own company. I will show you how this is done exactly.

There are people out there who specialize in building public shells and sell them to people who are looking to go public. You could learn how to do it and create 4 new shells per year and sell them $500,000 each. **You would easily make $2 million per year by simply doing this.**

Building your own sales organization to raise capital

Depending on your business model you might have built up a sales team that sells your products or services to clients. The sales that are generated help you to advance your business and therefore your company.

Depending on where you are in your development, you might not have enough money to move forward faster and expand your company.

> Besides getting money from financial companies, I would strongly suggest you build a second sales team who solely focuses on raising capital for your company.

When I first started my company, I actually had built up a separate company with 25 sales people who only contacted investors and raised capital for my deal. This sales organization became the driving force to finance my own deal and all they did all day was talk to potential investors. Because I owned this company, the sole purpose was to raise capital for my deal only and not for anybody else's deal. With this sales organization, I was able to raise $10 million alone in the first year.

Depending on your jurisdiction, your sales people might have to be licensed by the local authorities and pass an exam. It is even possible that your sales organization might have to be licensed as a financial company. But the advantage of having a company that only raises capital for your deals is priceless. It can make all the difference.

Your sales people will get paid a 10% commission from the money that they have raised themselves. The business basically finances itself based on the amount of money that you raise.

Even though this is a business on its own, you should look for a great sales manager who can run this business. This sales manager needs to be a bit of a drill sergeant because most sales people in this industry have mostly wild personalities.

Success is really easy when you think about it

Think about all the possibilities and options there are. If you don't believe that then you will be struggling your whole life. In the first world countries the money basically lies in the streets. You just have to do something and pick it up.

There are all kinds of options for you to make money in this world. We live in the richest and best time ever. Never before has it been easier to create wealth. Technology has made it possible for everyone with little or no money to create a business that can grow internationally. The Internet has opened up options that have never been there before.

To build a public company and to raise
money for it is possible for anyone.
All you need to have is an idea, a business plan, the right
set-up and then the skills to sell shares and raise capital.

Business Lessons

Not getting screwed in business

> "When doing business always act as if the other person
> is trying to screw you because most likely they are.
> And if they are not then you can be positively surprised."
> (Statement made by Steve Martin from
> the movie The Spanish Prisoner)

Unfortunately, all too often I have trusted people too much, given them control over accounts or I was too lazy to make a contract. Because I have a good heart and I want to believe in the good in people, I often got screwed.

When I heard this statement at first, I thought that it was too negative. But when you really think about it again, you will come to realize how much truth lies in this statement.

When dealing with a lot of money good people will turn bad very fast. Greed will take the better of them and then they start rationalizing why they deserve more and that you are all of a sudden the bad guy.

Lessons that I learned from running my own businesses

- Always make contracts even if you think you might not need them. The hurdle for someone to mess with you is a lot less if they know that you could legally take action because you have something in writing.
- Don't do too much work in advance for someone else. Always ask for a retainer. If someone can't pay you a

retainer then chances are that they can't pay you later anyway.

- Don't delay to get paid. Sometimes people tell you that the business needs the money more now than you do and that you will get paid later. Often this is a false conclusion because if the business cannot afford you now then there is something wrong with the set-up. Also if your payments are being delayed it might kill the business later on because the payment is going to be too large. So take the money off the table now!
- Don't ignore little signs. People don't change. If someone has ruined several businesses and has shown poor character with other people, chances are that sooner or later you will run into the same problems like they were.
- Some people have the tendency to over-promise and under-deliver. Don't get caught up in lies or exaggerations of someone. No one can do miracles and no one gives out money for nothing. So think and use common sense in every situation.
- You can delegate everything but never give away control over the finances. Whoever controls the money, controls the business.
- Try to identify BS (= bullshit) if you hear it. Often people tell you a lot of BS to try to convince you of something.
- Don't let yourself rush into something. Sometimes people try to urge you to do something and promise to pay you after. But because the situation seems to be urgent, they make you feel like you might miss out on an opportunity. The truth is that nothing is so urgent that it can't wait 24 or 48 hours. Do it like the Japanese: Tell them thank you but you want to sleep it over one night. Never get back to them after.

In the movie Scarface there was another interesting statement: "Don't underestimate the other guy's greed!" How true that is. Everybody is looking out for himself or herself and everybody is trying to make money. Don't be naïve to believe that others will do things out of the goodness of their hearts. Be smart and don't be too lazy to protect yourself.

Positive and important lessons

Courage

The number one quality for business success is courage. Never be afraid to ask. I believe that courage is the single most important factor in the beginning of any business venture. I called up some of the best geologists in the industry and asked them if they would join my team. Most of them had a PhD, were 30 years in the business and worked for the top companies in the world. To my surprise, most of them agreed because I simply asked.

Self-confidence

Many people laughed at us when we did our first presentations. They were even belittling us and tried to discourage us from our plan. But because we believed in ourselves and didn't listen to the negative people, we became great. Don't ever worry what other people are saying. Develop a clear vision, believe in yourself and follow through. If you don't believe in you, nobody else will.

Fake it until you make it

In the beginning when I tried to raise money, a lot of people laughed at me but as the organization grew, the same people started to admire me. Eventually, we got so much support from everybody around us, even the press, that people started to believe that we were in fact bigger than we actually were. But the more people start to believe in an idea, the more powerful this idea will be. You need to live your vision already today. If you want to become king one day, you already have to act like a king.

Pay yourself first

If you don't survive first, there is no company. You need to do well otherwise your company will never make it. If your company cannot afford to pay you a salary, then your whole concept is wrong. That is why I suggest that you always make sure that you get paid first and that you take money off the table when it is right. If you defer your payment to the future, it will eventually become a huge liability for the company and it will hurt the company and your reputation much more at a later point in time. It is totally ok to get paid for work that you have done.

Play in the big league

Why should you settle for a small time model? The rules for McDonald's and Coca Cola are the same like for your deal. So dream big and don't ever sell yourself short. Sometimes things can move really fast and catapult you into a higher category. Anything is possible in this business. Sometimes you get lucky with the right deal and get a huge financing at the same time. And it can all happen very quickly.

Never show any doubts

People don't follow anybody who has doubts. Don't ever communicate your doubts with anybody. The psychological factor of this is that you otherwise start to undermine your own self-confidence level and you give the wrong message to the Universe by pondering over your own doubts. If you have doubts, sit down and rewrite your plan of action. If you don't believe in yourself you can't expect others to believe in you.

> Laugh and the world will laugh with you.
> Weep and you weep alone.

Write in a daily journal

Before I became successful I listened to Brian Tracy, Anthony Robbins and many others. Every time I heard a good idea, I would write it into my book with empty pages. I started to gather ideas, make plans, put in my ideal business/work life and I wrote down my goals and dreams. I had really no idea what exactly my business would be doing but I knew HOW I wanted it to be organized, how many people I wanted to have working for me, what the colors of my logo would look like, etc. So when I actually started, I knew exactly, in advance, what the business would look like and because I had so much clarity in so many areas, I worked with the speed of light to make it happen. I had no doubts in my mind on how to do it and in return this gave off a vibe of self-confidence to others.

Control over money and accounts

This was one of my number one lessons. No matter who has the title of CEO, the person who has control over the money is really in charge. Do not ever give away that control. You can delegate everything but when it comes to money, you need to be the only person having access over the accounts, no matter how much you think you can trust a person. I paid dearly for this lesson and so have many others.

Work 10 to 12 hours each day

I consider myself a very efficient and intelligent person who can get a lot done in a very short period of time. I was never really a hard worker but a smart and efficient worker. But the lesson that I learned from my coach and friend David Garcia was to work more hours. I didn't want to believe it at first but when I embraced it, success started to happen. There are no two ways about it. Without putting in at least 10 to 12 hours a day you will never achieve financial success. David has a personal net worth of about $50 million.

There can only be one boss

As I have mentioned earlier. Partnerships don't work out. It is always a time bomb. Therefore you should only have a partner in business who is NOT doing the same as you. That is the only way. The only person in charge is you and only you should make major strategic decisions.

The reality principle

This is also a very sensitive issue for many people. Yes, you should dream big and be excited but at the same time you cannot live in la-la land as a businessperson. You always need to look at every situation with your "reality glasses". You need to honestly ask yourself what the REAL situation is like and not what you wish it to be. Only if you honestly assess and analyze it as it really is and not how you wish it were, can you make the necessary changes and preparations to make it happen. This is one of the most important lessons in business life. Without it, you are going to fail. It is a fine line between being negative and considering what could go wrong and having false optimism. That doesn't mean that you are a negative person. It means that your general motivation and outlook is still very positive but only if you find out what keeps you from not moving forward can you make real progress.

Clarity is key to success

Without clarity you end up nowhere. You need to define exactly and in detail what you want to achieve and then make a detailed plan to make it happen. So many people just try something out and then are baffled if they don't achieve their desired result. If you still have areas in your business where you are not 100% clear about the process and outcome you should sit down and get some clarity in those areas before you move forward.

Vision—dream big and make big plans

You can do, be or have anything in this life. Life is like a buffet. Everything is available, you just have to decide what you want. Don't ever sell yourself short and limit yourself because of low self-confidence. Create a big vision that excites you and even if it takes a lifetime to achieve it.

Encourage and motivate your people by giving them a vision where they have their role. Most people are not like you and never become leaders. But they can be a part of your vision and that will motivate them greatly.

Focus on sales and marketing

Everything in business has to do with selling and marketing. You should become an expert in sales and marketing no matter what your business does.

Don't try to be a perfectionist—80% is good enough

When I started with my first marketing material and brochures, they were not perfect but they were good enough to get the first few investors. With the money from the first few investors, I was able to hire a more professional marketing designer and have it printed on glossy paper. As things progressed, I would improve, rewrite or redesign all my materials. But if I had tried to get everything 100% perfect, I would have never started or gotten results.

To get momentum going, especially in the beginning, is crucial for your success and positive motivation. If you are going, you need to keep going. Don't try to be perfect; it will only slow you down. You can always improve things as you go along.

Get rid of people who emotionally block you

When I started a sales organization in the US I had hired about 15 sales people. Everybody was very motivated and full of positive expectations. But one person was a bad apple in the group. He started to talk negatively among his co-workers and he constantly challenged everybody and everything. He was very intelligent and had a lot of potential and I personally really liked him. However, he emotionally blocked the team and me. One day, I had to fire him because his energy was a bad influence for everybody. Even though there was nothing that he had done wrong, he was blocking me emotionally and my success. After I got rid of him, things moved forward again. Sometimes you need to get rid of people who are blocking you in life and in business. Not everybody is a good influence. My advice: Act fast when someone is not good for you. Don't wait too long.

Be a great communicator
95% of problems and misunderstandings have to do with bad communication and false expectations. Therefore, I recommend that you become a great communicator. Learn everything about this topic. The best book that I recommend to everybody is "How to win friends and influence people" by Dale Carnegie. This will not only improve your success in business and in sales but also in your personal relationships with your family and friends.

Failure is not an option—there is no plan B
If you go into something new and you don't go into it full heartedly you are more likely to fail. Be aware that if you leave options open so that, just in case, you can always go back to what you have done before, you are not convinced that you will succeed. You need to give a sign to the Universe saying something like this: "Hey Universe (or God) I am going to do this and I am going to succeed. There is no going back, ever." This can be done by doing an act of courage like renting a big office space that you intend to fill with people or something similar.

In battle, the ancient Greeks established a well-deserved reputation for bravery, discipline, and determination. They were successful because they were well-trained, well lead, and most of all, well motivated. The Greeks were master motivators who understood how to instill commitment and prepare their soldiers for victory. To infuse their army with a spirit of commitment, the moment they landed on the enemy's shore, the Greek commanders would give the order to "burn the boats." Imagine the tremendous psychological impact on the soldiers as they watched their boats being set to the torch. There was no turning back. Once their boats were burned, they realized that the only way they were going home was through victory.

<u>Be careful of people who only want to take advantage of you</u>
With success you will all, of a sudden, have a lot of new friends. Unfortunately, most people are not your real friends and will try to take advantage of you. So protect yourself from bloodsuckers. Also, be careful with whom you share sensitive information about your business and personal life. It's funny how people can change, all of a sudden, when money is involved. Their true nature and motivation will come to light. Also, I have met only very few people who are truly happy for your success. Most people are jealous or envious and talk badly behind your back. It is better to choose your close circle over time and with good care.

<u>Stay physically fit and healthy</u>
People who were once successful in sports tend to be successful in business later, too. It takes the same kind of character traits like self-discipline, working toward a goal, planning and many other things.

When you are working hard you will need a lot of mental, emotional and physical energy. By working out on a daily basis you ensure that you will feel better and have the necessary power to accomplish all your goals. Don't ever cut it out due to a busy schedule. Treat it like a scheduled appointment that you absolutely need to go to. Don't overthink it, either. Treat it like brushing your teeth every day. You just do it without thinking about it.

I would recommend doing it first thing in the morning when you get up. After it is done, you can go on with your workday.

Legal protection

Protect yourself legally all the time. Assume the other person or a client will one day try to come against you. Always have all angles covered as if you were preparing a court case to defend yourself. Gather all the proof and always get everything in writing; even if it doesn't appear to be important at first.

Enjoy the good things in life

Don't just work like a robot all the time. Enjoy the good things in life and give yourself a regular reward like booking a nicer hotel room or going out to eat in a great restaurant, for example. If you go on a business trip, add a couple of days to go sightseeing or rent a convertible sports car to get around.

If your subconscious mind is having fun and is getting rewards for doing all the hard work, it will continue to "support" you without having a burnout.

Achievement = happiness

I believe that people are the happiest when they are in the process of achieving their goals rather than having them achieved. It is during those times when you have your little successes and progress that will inspire you to continue going forward. Stop for a second and look how far you have come. Realize that you are in the process of getting it done and be happy NOW. Don't say things like: "Oh, only when I have achieved my goal, I will be happy." This is bad for your mental state and not true. Be grateful and happy now. Being in this exciting mission is what makes you happy.

Don't mix friends and business

It is important to have friends in your life that have absolutely nothing to do with your business. It is good to be surrounded by people who are not biased about some decisions and that can give you advice or help when you need it. Times are not always easy and you will need people in your life who are separate from your business.

Only work with people who have a good heart

I have worked with many people who were great sales people and who made me a lot of money. Unfortunately, some of them had bad intentions, a questionable integrity or had only their best interest at heart. After having dealt with too many of them in the course of my business life I came to the conclusion that I only want to be surrounded with people who have their heart in the right spot. It is far better to have someone working with you who has character and who has a good heart then someone who is only out for himself. Choose your people wisely and give them little "tests" here and there so you will see who they really are.

Lessons that I have learned in regards to Private Equity

Have always the majority of your deal

You always need to be in control of your deal. That is why you need to set it up the right way from the start. I would recommend issuing common shares for the investors and preferred shares for you. The preferred shares should have ten times the voting rights over common shareholders. This will ensure that you can always get rid of the management if necessary.

Be generous with your people but only issue options not stock

I used to make the mistake that I issued a million shares for someone in the beginning when I founded a company. Often, after a few months, that person was no longer in the business but still had a majority position in the deal and it was potentially hurting the deal. Therefore, I suggest that you always only issue options that are tied to specific milestones that help the business to move forward. For example, if you want to give someone one million shares so that he will get involved in your deal, you can make an agreement where you list 20 things that need to be accomplished during the next 12 to 24 months and each one of them is worth 50,000 shares. This way you will award the right amount of shares to the people who have helped the business to grow. And that if they still have shares, then it is fair and ok.

Sharks
Don't trust anybody when it comes to promotion. If you are entering the world of money and public companies, you should be aware that there are a lot of "sharks" out there. Almost everybody is promising you the world and in the end they only have their own interest at hand and not yours or the company's. Don't ever just issue shares to anyone in advance. Sometimes a stock promoter can kill your entire company by selling his own share position first and then your share price will drop to zero. Unfortunately, this was a lesson that I had to learn the hard way. Also be aware of lawyers that will overprice everything because you don't understand the process. Always get at least 3 different estimates.

Don't take every investor
One or two people out of a hundred are troublemakers. Usually it is a small investor who invests only about $5000. It is never the big ones who invest a few hundred thousand. The smaller investors will constantly give you trouble and threaten with legal action. Get rid of negative small investors with a bad attitude—you don't need the headache.

Communication with investors

Have a clear line of communication with investors—but not directly to you. If you are the CEO of the company you have a lot of things to take care of. It is better to have sales people or an investor relations department who will deal with questions and problems of investors. If you deal with everybody you will never get anything done for your business. Also, if you need to make an unpopular decision, you don't need the negative energy constantly to discourage you to take action.

Things and times change

Be flexible and change your approach if things are not working as they used to. Sales and marketing approaches that used to work five years ago will have changed. If you were able to get sales the old fashioned way and it is no longer working, then change your approach. Too many cold calls from companies who are selling their products over the phone have annoyed people and made it almost impossible to do cold calling. Too many spam email messages make it difficult to get your message across. So re-think everything and analyze what works today.

The business of getting investors

Getting the Money You Need to Finance Your Business

If you are starting your own business you will need money. Depending on your business idea you might not have the necessary funds to realize your idea.

Most people think that they need to get a loan from a bank to get started. They soon realize that banks are not willing to lend money without any collateral. Very often this marks the end of most business dreams.

Another way to finance your business idea is to get money from private investors. We have seen a lot of people with great business ideas struggle to get money from investors. The problem was often that..

1. They either had no clear strategy on how someone could invest into their business
2. The investor would take over too much ownership of the business or
3. There was no clear exit strategy for the investor to be motivated enough to invest in the first place.

If you expect someone to invest into your company simply because you think it is a great company but you don't make it clear what percentage someone can obtain, how long he must expect to stay invested, how much the annual return on the investment will be or how many times over the investment could multiply, and finally, how and when exactly someone can expect to get his or her investment back, it won't happen.

Even though this sounds like common sense, most people who are looking for money have no clear strategy when it comes to this.

The solution is called "private equity". A business should be set up from the start in such a manner that there is a structure and plan for investors to be able to buy shares of the company. There needs to be a clear share structure in place so that the owner of the business does not lose control but at the same time allows investors to participate.

The main idea is for the investor to buy shares in your company at a low and attractive price and over the course of 12 to 24 months there should be an IPO so that the investor can sell his shares in the market for a higher price.

The most important factor for investors is the exit strategy and the potential return on their investment. If you can show or predict how much money they are going to make by investing into your company and when they can expect to get their returns, only then will they be motivated to invest in the first place.

The offering and share structure

In order to raise money from investors you need to have a clear plan in advance. You should put together a share structure of how many shares will be sold to investors and how many shares will stay in the hands of the founders.

A basic plan could look like this:

	Shares issued	Price	Capital raised
Founders	20 million shares	$0.0001	$2000

1st round	5 million shares	$0.10	$500,000
2nd round	5 million shares	$0.20	$1 million
3rd round	5 million shares	$0.50	$2.5 million
First price when trading		$1.00	

The total amount of money that you will raise will be $4 million (plus $2000) and 35 million shares will be issued.

The goal is to use the $4 million to go public and to develop the business model.

You will need to put together a PPM (Private Placement Memorandum) and inform the SEC by filing a Form D to announce your intention to raise capital and to go public. You need to do this within 15 days of getting your first investor. You will have to use an SSA (Share Subscription Agreement), which is a legal contract to sell your shares.

With a clear plan and structure you will know exactly how much you will need to sell and at what price. Develop a clear exit strategy for your investors. This will help in your process to raise money.

Selling stocks is no different than selling any other product— it is all sales!

The people who make most money in this business are the people who are very good at sales. This means that they are very good in dealing with other people, they understand exactly what kind of concerns and objections clients have, they are basically psychologists in disguise who know a lot of techniques to influence other people. If used with integrity then they help other people to make the right decisions and to get them to move from the security based low performance thinking into better choices.

Everything is a numbers game

Selling a product or service has a lot to do with the law of probability. Whatever it is that you sell, it is always a numbers game. That means that you might have to offer your product or service to many prospective clients in order to make a sale.

So the more people you talk to, the more sales you will make. You can literally calculate how much money you want to make. Selling is like math.

You need to define the steps that it takes before a client buys a product. This could look something like this: You initially send out a letter to clients. Then you call them up and try to get an appointment. At the appointment you make a presentation and then a certain number of people will buy your product. You might start out with a hundred names, get twenty appointments and close seven sales. Your overall sales closing rate is 7% in this example.

The sales funnel

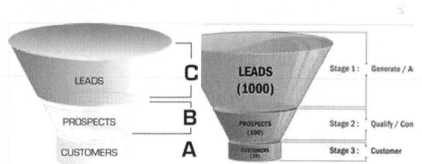

Try to think in numbers when it comes to your business. You need to be able to calculate the number of efforts it takes in order to achieve an end result.

You might have to talk to 1000 people first before you can make a sale. There is always somebody who will buy your product. The only question is which sales channels work better and what you can do to improve the individual steps in your sales process to get better numbers. The more people that come into contact with your product or service, the more sales you will have in the end. This is the law of probability.

The founder of Starbucks had spoken to over 256 people about investing into his business. Only 12 people ended up doing it. He was rejected over 240 times but his persistence paid off in the end.

So if your product can be sold and the result is in reasonable proportion to the efforts that you have to put forth, it is only a matter of the amount of acquisition efforts that you have to do in order to be successful.

> The only person standing in your way might be yourself. If you are not lazy or afraid of rejection, there is no limit to what you can achieve.

The psychology of the sales funnel might be tricky. You might have spoken to 50 people on the phone and gotten rejected each time and therefore you conclude that no one wants to buy your product. Often people give up way too easily and early because they are afraid of rejection and they don't see the bigger picture. The truth is that they simply haven't spoken to enough people to make that assessment or they are using the wrong technique to go about their business.

Many paths lead to Rome

There is not just one way to get investors. There are several ways you can find clients:

1. Telephone sales—cold calling
2. Personal network and existing relationships
3. Public presentations
4. Working with other intermediaries or advisors who already have clients and contacts
5. Internet marketing strategies
6. Other ways (more later)

In general, you need to be able to develop a trust relationship with a person so that he will make an investment. Without trust, there is no sale. You will always have better chances if you can have a face-to-face meeting with someone. Selling over the phone is also very possible but it is a different process and more of a numbers game.

Selling stock over the phone and creating clients

> The idea is to create a system that initially generates new leads – not clients!

No one will buy something on the first phone call. Especially when it comes to investing.

The first point of contact has to be a non-threatening experience for the prospect. Only after a prospect feels comfortable and has developed trust with the sales person, then he will invest.

I am going to show you how we operated and created clients with our system to sell stocks over the phone.

1st phone call: Marketing call—cold call (marketing position— typically a woman)

The main goal is to get people to agree to receive general marketing information about your company for free and without any obligation. It is important to identify those people who show a general interest in investing in the type of products that your company offers.

I have hired 5 women who spend 5 hours each day on the phone using lists from the phone book of certain professions making 200 calls each per day.

Based on the quality of the list that they are calling, they generate an average of 5 people who are willing to receive the information and therefore become "leads".

A conversation could go something like this:

Hi, I am calling from XYZ Company. We would like to introduce ourselves and our company to you. We are a company specializing in ABC investments and we help companies to go public. We would like to send you some general information about our company by email so that you can see whether this could be of interest to you or not. We are currently working on deal ABC that will go public in 6 months and it is a very interesting investment opportunity because we can currently offer the shares at $0.50 and we expect the company to be valued at $2.00 when it is listed. All we want to do is to send you some general information about his deal so that you can take a look at it. What is your email address please?

An experienced broker will give you a call in a few days after you had the chance to review the information and he will be able to answer any questions that you might have.

One more question: If you like what we have to offer, would you be able to invest anywhere from $50,000 to $100,000?

The goal of each marketing person is to generate at least 5 new leads per day. By working 5 hours a day, five days a week and 4 weeks per month, they generate at least 100 leads per month.

Experience shows that out of 100 leads, you will get about 2 to 3 clients.

The better the quality of leads, the more sales can be done.

By a good quality lead I mean the following things:

1. The investor has the ability to invest. He has enough money available to make an investment now.
2. The investor has been informed about the deal and has a general idea what the investment opportunity is all about.
3. The amount of the investment is high. The higher the better, of course.
4. The investor is open to discuss investments on the phone.
5. The investor shows a general interest in your topic and company.

So the better the first call goes, the better the lead will be. It is important that the prospect is well informed in general what the second call will be all about. This will make the broker's job much easier.

2nd call: Follow up call from broker (different person)

A broker or experienced sales person will make the second call and follow up with the client. The goal is to develop trust and give the client more information about the product. The goal is to sell him on the idea and motivate him to make an investment.

Usually, a client will not be ready to make an investment right then and there. That is why your goal will be to provide him with more information and maybe even to send him a contract for his review.

3rd call: Closing time

The purpose now is to answer any objections or concerns that the investor might have about the deal and to get the investment. Since the level of trust is still small, the investor might do a trial investment of $5000 to $10,000 initially. This will establish the relationship and trust level.

4th call: Loading the client

Once the client has developed an initial relationship with the broker and has agreed to invest into the deal, the investment can be increased. Most people who start out investing $10,000 will eventually increase their investment to $50,000 or $100,000 if there is still a positive development in the company and he can still get a good price on the acquisition of the shares.

Building a sales team

Having a business means nothing else than selling your products or services to customers to make a profit. The more products you sell, the higher is your profit.

There is only so much time in a day and so much effort that you can put into selling the products yourself. That is why you need to get additional help or leverage. Ten people will sell much more than you will be able to sell. If you build a sales team you can focus on improving the company and its products.

The key to building a sales team is to find a good sales manager first. This person must be an experienced sales person who knows everything about selling and can train and motivate other people.

You should focus your efforts on getting as many sales people as possible. Create a sales organization that is motivating and that will not make you go broke. You can have people on straight commission or organize the sales team in such a way that you ensure by the law of averages that a certain amount of sales is inevitable.

You can create two types of sales teams. First, there are the sales people that actually sell the product that your company has to offer. And second, you can create a sales team that only raises money by selling shares of the company to investors.

Building a sales team is easier than you think. There are a lot of people out there that would like to improve their lives and make more money. You can offer them a job with the opportunity to make a lot of commission and at the same time they help you to achieve your business goals.

You need to rent an office with several phone lines and then you will be amazed how much faster and bigger your results will be.

You can pay $10 per hour per person who is doing marketing calls. I would also add a certain percentage 2-5% of the sales commission to motivate them to make more calls. If they get the right clients prepared who will do a big investment, the bigger will their own paycheck be.

Let's do the math:

You could hire 10 marketing sales people and you pay them $10 per hour. If they work 5 hours per day, 5 days a week and 4 weeks a month, your cost per person will be $1000 in base salary.

10 marketing sales people will cost you $10,000 per month. Office rent and expenses might also add another $5000 and therefore your operation will cost you $15,000 per month.

But what will be the benefit? You should create 1000 new leads for new potential clients each month. If you can turn 10% of those leads into 100 good prospects and you only close 20% of those prospects, you will create 20 new clients per month.

Now, based on the quality and ability of your clients to make an investment, you could have a conservative average investment of $10,000 per client, which will lead to an overall investment of $200,000 per month.

The $200,000 will go directly into the bank account of the company. It is there where you can deduct the $15,000 investment as a marketing expense to finance your sales team.

$15,000 plus 10% in commissions for the sales people will end up costing the company $35,000 per month. But the amount of investments that you have received will be well worth it.

If you intend to raise $2 million in the first year to finance your projects and take your company public, you will be able to accomplish this with hiring a sales and marketing team of 10 people.

Math backwards

A broker or sales person should have a clear plan on how much money he wants to raise and how much money he wants to earn.

Example:

A broker wants to make $250,000 per year in personal income. If he earns a 10% commission, he needs to raise $2.5 million from investors for the company. That means that he needs to raise an average amount of about $200,000 per month.

He can do it the following ways:

- 1 client with 1 investment of $200,000
- 2 clients with an investment of $100,000 each
- 10 clients with an investment of $20,000 each
- 20 clients with an investment of $10,000 each
- A mix of different amounts

Based on his strategy he has to target different clients. If he only needs one investment of $200,000 per month, he should only focus on people who are very wealthy.

If he wants to get 10 to 20 clients who will make a smaller investment, his approach will be a bit differently.

Personal face-to-face meetings

The best way to get clients is in a face-to-face meeting. If you can sit down with a client and show him a power point presentation about your company and you get to go through all the positive reasons why an investment makes sense, you will be a good chance of closing a deal.

Typically, I would put together a power point presentation in the following manner:

1. Small talk and assessing the clients situation and mood
2. Goals and dreams: Talk about what goals and dreams that he has in his life.
3. Start with investments in general and compare all options.
4. Come to the conclusion that stocks have the best performance in the long run.
5. Explain why smaller stocks outperform larger stocks
6. Explain how a pre-IPO stock performs even better and give examples
7. Talk about the industry that your product is in.
8. Talk about the reasons why it makes sense to be invested in this industry.
9. Present the company and conclude that it fulfills all the factors that you were talking about earlier and that he can achieve his goals and dreams with this investment.
10. Ask for an investment.

Another strategy for a personal meeting could be the one that financial planners use. Financial Planners first gather all the financial information about a client. They use a questionnaire to find out what the client's needs are. Then they go back to the office and make a general financial analysis. They meet the client for a second time and present solutions about how to save taxes, change insurances, save money and how to improve their investments.

You could offer clients to check out their portfolios and you give them free advice on what to change or improve. By doing so you can suggest that he will invest a certain amount into Private Equity—meaning the shares that you are selling.

In general, investing into a Private Equity investment should not exceed more than 5-10% of someone's overall portfolio.

Personal network and existing relationships

When you start out in this business you should sit down for about 2 to 3 hours and compile a list of absolutely all contacts that you have. You will realize that you will have at least 200 to 300 contacts of people that you know personally. That is a good start.

At the end of this program you will find the memory jogger. This is a list of all possible connections and groups so that you will be able to do your brainstorming to create your initial list of contacts.

Not everybody on your list will become a client. That is not possible. But some will. People who already know you and trust you are a good start to begin selling to. You will get more comfortable with the process and by making your first sales you will build up your self-confidence and momentum.

After you have identified who could possibly become a client, you should also consider people who could give you referrals or other contacts. Some of those people might not be an investor but they do know a lot of other people. It is much easier to call up a stranger if you can refer to a friend that you have in common. It will open the door much easier for you.

When I tried to finance my first deal I wrote 50 letters to my contacts. I explained on two pages what I was trying to do and that I would contact them. 3 out of those 50 people actually contacted me and told me that they would give me some money to invest. The other people I contacted personally and set up individual meetings where I explained what the company did. This gave me a great start and some money for my company.

Working with other intermediaries or advisors who already have clients and contacts

There are some investment advisors that are one man shows. They typically have about 100 to 200 clients and manage between $50 and $200 million for their clients. Those investment advisors usually get an annual management fee of about 2% for managing the client's portfolio and maybe even a performance fee if the portfolio does well. Some of those advisors are happy and very motivated to get 10% commission for selling your shares to their clients.

This can actually be a great way of getting clients. The only person that you need to convince is the advisor and he will do the selling to his clients for you. Since he will get a commission for it, he will make money and everybody wins.

Sometimes those independent investment advisors can raise easily several hundred thousand dollars for you in a matter of a couple of weeks. If you focus your efforts on building 10 to 20 connections like that, you will have enough money raised for your company.

But there is also an important warning: Some advisors like tax consultants, bankers or brokers will not be helpful and actually trash your product. The reason is because they cannot legally get a commission and if they advise the client to invest and the investor loses money, they could become liable or lose their reputation.

Some broker dealers in America are legally not allowed to sell the shares of your private placement unless their compliance officer has approved your product. Often, they will not be able to approve your product anyway because FINRA's rules and standards will make it almost impossible for them. Too many things are unstable with start-up companies and the risk might be too high for most investors. So don't waste your time on professional brokers.

If you want to make a deal with a brokerage or a private equity firm, they will usually want to restructure your company's share structure and they will take about 80% of the ownership in return of giving you money. Don't even waste your time there.

Depending on the country that you are selling your shares from you need to be aware of the financial laws on who is legally able to sell shares. In the US someone needs to be licensed with a broker dealer and have a Series 7 and 63/65 license. All other people are legally not allowed to sell shares.

BUT there is one exception: If you are the president or a director of the company you are legally able to raise capital and sell shares of your own company. So if you have some sales people that help you raise capital for your deal, you will have to make them directors of the company so that they are not violating any securities laws. In most European countries financial advisors simply need to be members of a SRO (self-regulatory organization). The laws vary from country to country. But as a DIRECTOR of the company you can always sell. It is actually your job and obligation to help to progress the company.

Public presentations

Another great way to get clients is to organize a monthly or weekly presentation in a hotel. You could advertise a free presentation or seminar with the following topics:

- Make money with private equity
- Creating wealth by investing smart
- Investment strategies to help you save taxes
- Improve your overall portfolio with private equity investments
- Oil and gas—a thriving industry
- Make more money with new trading strategies
- Gold expert John Smith will talk about global gold development

The idea is to present a seminar on a specific topic that people want to hear about. You should not advertise your own company. You could even hire an expert in your field who will give a speech. At the end of your presentation he will then talk about your product for about 5 minutes and recommend it.

Your job now is to follow up with all the people who showed up to the seminar and set up meetings.

Monthly company presentations

Once a month I would organize a company presentation in a hotel. I would call up existing investors to give them an update and invite prospects who were on the fence about investing. I usually invited the head geologist to talk about the development of the gold exploration projects. I would also invite potential clients who would hear the story for the first time.

Typically, I would invite about 10 to 20 people for a 90-minute presentation and raise about $200,000 to $300,000 each time. It was a great way to raise capital from existing and new potential investors.

Internet marketing strategies

Another great way to creating leads is the Internet. You should create a website and offer a free report about investing into private equity in general. People who would request the report would get a call from the women in your marketing call center. They would ask if the person is interested in receiving an actual deal that refers to Private Equity.

A sales letter that you can send out on the Internet typically precedes the report. The goal is to generate leads initially and not clients. But it will fill your sales funnel with potential new clients.

Intermediaries or contacts in foreign countries

You might not be able to speak Russian or Chinese but you might have one contact person locally in a foreign country that has a lot of connections. You could arrange a commission agreement for 10% with that person to refer clients to you. Depending on your contact this person might have great connections and investors.

You might also consider countries or markets like South America, for example. You might not be able to speak Spanish perfectly but someone else here in America can. They might target clients all over the world of countries that are looking for investment opportunities or options to invest their money in America.

The only person that you would be dealing with is your one connection.

Mutual Funds, hedge funds or other investment vehicles

Normally, I would not encourage you to target big financial firms or investment funds. Based on their strategy and rules they might not be allowed to invest into a company like yours because of the risk factors.

However, when I was doing a gold deal, I targeted gold funds. I actually found one gold fund in Liechtenstein that ended up investing more than $2 million into my company.

95% of those companies will not invest into your company because it is too small, too risky or not developed enough. Most funds can only invest into public companies anyway so you should only approach them once your company is listed. But there might be a small percentage that can make an investment. Typically, it is smaller independent investment funds or hedge funds. You could even offer additional shares to the fund manager personally so that he can either benefit himself or minimize the risk of the investment to justify it with his board.

Other shareholder lists

The best potential investors are people who have already invested in a similar type of investment once before. Those lists are valuable like gold. Typically, the personality of the people on those lists is risky because they are gamblers by nature. Even if they have lost money in a deal before, they are very likely to invest in another risky venture again because they want to believe in making the big buck.

Target market—Ideal client to make an investment

The better you can identify your ideal investor, the better you can market to that group. My experience shows the following investors' criteria:

1. 40 to 70 years of age
2. Business owners or self-employed people
3. Middle management of big companies with good salaries
4. Less experienced investors who are not financial experts
5. A profession that makes good money (like specialists, doctors, etc.)

20 marketing sales people in a third world country

Based on the clients that you will target you could set up a call center in a foreign country. At one point we have only targeted investors in the German speaking part of Europe (Germany, Austria and Switzerland) because the financial potential was much better at the time than in America.

In Europe, a lot of people speak several languages. We have had a marketing team of women who call up clients in Germany from an Eastern European country because the costs of running an operation in those countries are much cheaper.

A person in the US would get a salary around $1000 per month. A person in Eastern Europe would only be about $300 to $400 per month.

If you hire 20 people who will work in your call center and generate leads every day you will have so many leads and clients that you won't be able to manage them all. The key to running a successful organization like that is one person locally who is managing the team on a daily basis. If you can find that ONE person who is the tough sergeant in the call center and who is making sure that plenty of calls are done, then you got it made.

Based on your strategy you could do it for other countries as well provided you will have the right sales people who will be able to close in the local language.

One more important piece of advice: It is much better to have foreign investors than US investors in a deal. If the stock does not go as planned, you can avoid a lot of legal problems and headaches. The SEC is not interested in making sure that foreigners are protected. The SEC only cares about US investors. Of course, you want to make sure to always follow the law properly and do your best to always act with the highest integrity. In that case you have nothing to worry about.

Marketing strategies are constantly changing

One of the most important points is copying successful strategies. If you do what other companies have done you should get the same results. You don't need to figure it out by yourself first and fall on your face when you get started. Apply the same successful strategies.

It is also important to understand that marketing strategies are constantly changing. If things have worked a few years ago they might not work today. An example of this is email blast marketing. Because people were spammed so much they refuse to read any messages from unknown senders or they automatically go into a spam folder.

The goal in marketing is to understand human behavior and apply strategies that target basic human needs like love, beauty, relationships, money and recognition.

Another important factor is a first unthreatening possibility of contact. Some people don't want to talk to a sales person because they are afraid of being talked into something that they don't really want. Offer your potential clients the opportunity to get information about your product and services that is risk or pressure free.

Selling in general

> Every business transaction has to do with selling.

When it comes to selling shares, it doesn't really matter what the company is doing as a business model. People make buying decisions based on the sales person and how much you were able to develop trust.

In the end, you need to sell yourself and the things that your customers wants. Typically, those things are more money, feeling safe, feeling smart about the investment, doing the right thing, greed, fear of loss, diversification and various other reasons.

Your main focus should be on how to generate more sales or customers. Therefore you should become an expert in sales and marketing.

For some people selling has a negative association. The truth is, however, that every businessman or woman is primarily a sales person even if you don't have the title sales rep on your card. You have to constantly keep selling your person to your clients, to your boss, your spouse and the people around you. No matter what you do you need to sell yourself all the time. That is why it is important to learn everything there is to know about selling and communication.

I encourage you to embrace the world of selling and find new joy in becoming better each day.

You need to become a master at marketing and sales. Actually, every one of us is already an expert. You are being bombarded daily with offers and people who try to sell something to you. Instinctively, you know what works and what doesn't. Often, common sense is a better judge than any fancy strategy that someone tries to teach you.

Marketing is something that can be learned. Read and learn everything that you can about marketing and sales. Become the best at it. You need to learn and understand the psychology of people, what makes them tick and how to best present your products.

There are hundreds of great books about this subject. Selling is not bothering people and trying to sell them something that they don't need but rather the art of helping people get what they want.

Building a client list

It is important that you look at your business in numbers. Here are the possibilities to increase your sales:

1. Increase your average sale
2. Increase the number of clients
3. Increase the number of transactions per client per year

You should be aware that you don't need the whole world as clients in order to be successful. If you have a hundred clients, you will never have to worry again. In some businesses you will need a lot less.

You should start by creating a database with all the people that you know. You should gather names and use all your contacts to expand your list. The longer your list is to start out, the better. Your initial list should contain at least 200 to 300 contacts.

If you had a hundred clients who buy once a year from you, you will have enough to make a good living. If your success rate to get new clients is 10% you will need 1000 names to reach your goal.

If you increase the average transaction per client to twice a year and increase the average transaction size, your income will triple.

> Everything is based on numbers and the
> amount and quality of your contacts.

In order to be successful, you need to lose all your fears and aggressively start selling and promoting your products. By aggressive I don't mean being rude and annoying. Aggressive means to be very active and to talk to as many people about your products as you possibly can. Make a commitment to never be lazy!

A famous quote by Robert Half goes like this:

> "Laziness is a secret ingredient that goes into failure.
> But it is only kept secret from the person who fails."

Many shortcomings can be overcome if you are actively speaking to different people. There will always be a certain percentage of people that will always buy your products. Especially in the beginning you need the momentum to keep going and stay motivated.

For one of our companies, for example, we held a monthly presentation in a hotel. Usually, we had about 10 to 20 people attending the presentation. It was an investors' presentation to get them to invest into our company. Each time we were able to raise about $200,000 to $300,000 per presentation. This gave us the necessary capital to continue with our operations. It was not our only source of investors' money of course because we were active in all the possible venues. We made phone calls, we had meetings with professional investment advisors and we sent out monthly newsletters.

Whatever you do you should spend 80% of your time selling, promoting and presenting.

Potential clients

Go to a public place like the mall or a concert and ask yourself what kind of success you would have if only every tenth person were buying your products. You need to open yourself up to the endless possibilities that this world offers.

You will realize that you can only handle so much and that the world is too big to sell your products to everybody. Therefore you need to clearly define your absolute target customer. Who is your customer? What age group does he ideally belong to? Which magazines does your customer read? Which places does your customer go? The more clearly you can define who your ideal customer is the more effective will your marketing efforts be.

Building a client database

The number one goal of your business should be to build up a certain number of clients over a specific amount of time. For example, you could have the goal to build up 500 clients over the course of the next five years.

Once you have built up such a client database you will never have to worry again how to produce sales. A good client list is valuable like gold. A single marketing action can immediately produce results and generate income.

Depending on the business you might be able to live comfortably with only 200-300 good clients. In case you ever decided to sell your company to someone else, your client list is one of your biggest assets. Therefore, protect it and make sure your competitors or employees don't steal it.

Using referrals—cold calling vs. warm leads

One of the best ways to build your business is to ask for referrals. If you always ask for referrals each time you deal with a client you can continually grow your business. The important thing is to really ask every single person you come in contact with whether they have become a client or not.

In America people have been bombarded by sales people and automated systems for the last twenty years. Everyone is used to getting several sales calls per week from various companies and sometimes people get talked into buying products that they don't really need.

Cold calling has been overdone and people in America are tired of sales people trying to sell them something. They get angry and annoyed when yet another person is trying to sell them something over the phone. Most people are so fed up with the extreme overload of sales calls that they simply hang up the phone when someone is trying to talk to them or the get really rude.

Because of this phenomenon, clients have installed caller ID systems on their phones and they don't even answer the phone is they see that the number is either blocked or unknown.

For the sales person or business owner on the other hand, cold calling has become increasingly difficult and frustrating because he gets less and less chances to talk to prospects.

Traditional cold calling is a numbers game. The more calls you make, the more prospects you will have. But if you cannot get a hold of people and if you don't get a chance to talk to people, the time spent cold calling is not in relation to the results that you desire. There is always a percentage of people who will turn into prospects but with today's technology and people's annoyance this percentage has gone down tremendously.

In most businesses, you need to talk to as many people as possible to turn names into prospects and finally into clients. By trying to do cold calling like everybody else, you decrease the efficiency to getting clients. Even though you might have great things to offer, you need to be able to get your message out to the public. If the people knew what you know, they would not hang up on you. Therefore, the traditional cold calling process does not seem to be the best way anymore.

In Switzerland, I used to work for the biggest independent financial planning company in Europe. The only way that we would get clients was strictly through referrals from existing clients. Nobody would even consider doing cold calling because the time and effort spent on cold calling was way too much compared to the seemingly easy way of calling people when being referred to them.

Calling someone by referral is still the process of calling up a stranger and asking him to become a prospect. But the main difference is that because the sales person can say that a mutual friend has referred him, the trust level is already 50% established and therefore the willingness for the prospect to proceed is much higher.

Making phone calls by using referrals is so much easier than cold calling and much more effective. The willingness to listen to you is much greater because their friend has referred them to you. If your friend referred you to someone, you would at least listen. Also, the level of trust is much higher because your friend would never refer somebody to you if it weren't a good product.

Applying the numbers game by utilizing referrals also results in much better numbers. The percentages go up and the time spent making phone calls goes down. Your motivation to make phone calls each day is much greater because you know that your efforts will lead to meetings or results. If you had to do cold calling, you can easily get discouraged because of the low success rate. Therefore, never do cold calling. Always call people if you have a referral or a reference. You will be able to build your business much faster and more efficient like this.

The best way to get started is by writing down every contact that you have yourself. Make a list of at least 100 people that you know personally. Contact each one of them and either set up a short meeting or talk to them on the phone. Ideally, you want to get a meeting with the 20 most important people on your list, to get 20-30 referrals from each person. The goal should be to accumulate at least 500 new names (referrals) that will be the foundation of your career. After you have your 500 names, you can start making calls and get the people into the sales funnel.

It is important to always ask for referrals in every meeting. Get used to asking for referrals and use your referral sheet. The more referrals you have, the less cold calling you need to do and the more meetings you can schedule.

Writing a sales letter

One of the best sales tools is writing a sales letter. It can be sent out on paper or by email. A sales letter is basically nothing else than a sales presentation in a written form that should motivate a potential client to buy your product that lists all the advantages and answers all the potential questions and concerns that people might have.

It contains a lot of psychological basics and is usually structured in an easy to read format. It typically starts with a general problem that a client would like to solve and ends with the solution. It is presented in such a way that the value of the product far exceeds the price. It is written with lots of emotional statements and will influence a potential customer to buy the product.

Studies have shown that a longer sales letter that is between ten and twenty pages long will outperform short brochures that are only one or two pages.

If you don't have the best writing skills, you could also hire a professional writer.

What motivates and drives people—greed

In the movie "Wallstreet" there was a famous scene where Michael Douglas as Gordon Gecko said: Greed is good.

No matter what you might want to believe, but there is a lot of truth in that statement when you apply it to investors. In today's world, most people want something for nothing and they want to make it big. A lot of people are still looking for the one miracle investment that will make them rich in very short period of time. Because we all have heard stories of people who picked the right stock and it went through the roof.

For the longest time I refused to believe that most people were driven by greed. I believed it to be a myth and a negative way of thinking. I decided to offer two different kinds of products to my clients. One product had a 100% capital guarantee with an interesting structure and great possible performance and the other product was purely speculative, high risk but also with a high reward potential. Guess what most people chose? Not one person wanted the product with the capital guarantee. They all wanted the risky deal.

It is psychologically interesting that people's common sense and reason will shut down when they believe that they can make 1000%. No one will believe you that you can make 50% because they think it is fishy but when you mention that they can make 10x more with their money, they all become greedy.

Since I have consulted thousands of clients in the course of my career and sold them conservative and stable products, I have decided to solely focus on dynamic investments like private equity and public stocks of start up companies. It is a lot more fun and the potential for making money for your investors is also much greater.

DO NOT TRY: Inefficient ways of trying to get investors

LinkedIn:
LinkedIn is a platform where professionals can post their profile. There is even a group of people who call themselves investors. At first it seems like a great idea but the reality is that it is a waste of time. Most people present themselves better than they actually are and people with money do not post their profiles online telling the whole world that they are looking for investments. Think about it. It doesn't make sense. A former employee of mine spent 6 months communicating with so called potential investors and never made a single sale.

Facebook and Twitter:
People don't want to be bothered with sales offers online. It is not recommended as a constant strategy. You might get a couple of clients in the beginning because they know you personally but it is not a strategy to be used for your business to get investors. The only way you can use it is for marketing your investment company but not for specific investments.

Mixers and networking meetings
That is the biggest waste of your time. People who go to those meetings are usually looking for clients or money because they have no money themselves. A successful person who is busy and successful doesn't have time to waste with mixers.

Bankers, accountants or financial advisors
Typically not a good source because they are bound to a lot of laws that will not enable them to do business with you. Usually, those "professionals" will belittle you or your deal because it is

too new and risky. Meetings with people like that can rob you of your motivation. Don't let that happen. You will get enough rejection as it is.

A person on the street, in a restaurant or the hairdresser or at the gym

It is possible to meet people to which you can develop a good rapport and get them as clients. But it is quite unprofessional and not a strategy that you use to build your business. You might get lucky and get a couple of clients but soon you will run out of steam because you won't be able to generate sales on a consistent basis.

Cold calling all day without strategy or target group

This is typically a waste of your time, energy and motivation. Without a strategy or specific plan you won't achieve anything. If you target a specific group by calling a list you need to use a referral mechanism. You could, for example, join the horse club of Del Mar and then call up all members. But you would have to announce yourself as a member first so that they would be open to listen to you.

Financial institutions and mutual funds that are too large

All financial institutions or mutual funds have specific rules of what they are allowed to invest in and what they cannot do. Typically, they won't be able to invest into a new start-up company.

People who ask for a retainer

There are a lot of people who promise you to get your company financed because they have such an extensive personal network to financial institutions. If they ask for a retainer, run or hang up the phone. Most of those people are in the business of making a living with people who will pay them a retainer. Each time I hired someone and paid them a fee or a retainer, it ended up being a disaster. So don't do it.

Direct mail, ads, flyers, etc.
Those things are not efficient and a waste of time, money and energy. Besides, it is illegal to promote the sale of shares to private investors in America.

Email campaign or promotion on the Internet
Raising money publicly is illegal in the US. The law states that you need to have a preexisting relationship with the client and that it is unsolicited. Also, because you are trying to sell shares privately and not through a regulated stock market, you are acting under an exemption. You will jeopardize your whole company if you start publicly promoting your company's shares and offering if the SEC or FINRA will find out. There is a new change in the law that will allow you to do certain things in the near future but please consult with a securities lawyer about the details.

Other ways to get investors

Clubs and associations
Join an organization, club or religious group and get the contact list of all members. If people can associate with you and you can call them up because you are in the same organization, they will at least listen to you.

Churches
If you are a member of a church and a person of integrity you will be surprised to see how much support you can get from your church. A former employee of mine raised over $500,000 alone in one week from the people of his church.

Other people with lists (e.g. real estate agents)

Sometimes it can make sense to exchange lists with another professional like, for example, a real estate agent. The target group is pretty much the same and you can help each other to refer business.

Writing a PR article yourself or your company

Depending on the company that you are raising money for, it might make sense to get an article about your company published. This will add credibility and get people interested in your deal.

Getting on TV

If your company has very special or interesting products that are unusual, they might get coverage from a TV station. This could give you a lot of attention and therefore clients.

Contact angry client that you lost

You would be surprised to see how can turn around an angry client if you contact him or her again. 50% of angry clients will stay angry but the other 50% simply want to be heard and taken seriously. By taking the courage to call them you will be able to turn some clients from the negative into the positive.

Not interested clients

Call everybody who was not interested again in 3 months. Typically, they said that they were not interested because the might have been busy at the time of your call, under stress or simply in a bad mood. You can often get people interested if you catch them at the right time.

Openness, honesty, integrity and transparency

In my opinion, you will have the best chance of getting investors to invest into your company if you are open and honest about everything. Even if things are not perfect yet and you communicate it properly to your potential investors, they will appreciate your integrity and transparency.

A survey has shown that the number one quality that clients look for in sales people is honesty.

Obviously, you want to put your company is the best possible light but don't be afraid to admit things that are not yet where they should be.

If you are an entrepreneur who has a vision and a dream, you will attract investors with the fire and excitement that is inside of you. Remember always: if the idea is good, then the money will follow. Lack of money initially is not a reason why a new venture will not work. There are always people out there who are willing to bet on the underdog.

Be very self-disciplined whether you feel like working or not

The key to raising money is self-discipline. You need to follow a clear plan and strategy that you will execute every day. You will need to apply the numbers game and focus all your energies on executing your tasks that will get you new investors.

Your personal commitment will determine whether you will achieve your goals or not. Everybody will have a bad or unlucky day once in a while. But if you keep doing the things that have proven to work and you continue to do them, then you will eventually reach your goals. So don't ever give up.

There is no such thing as luck. The harder you work, the luckier you will get. The more opportunities that you create the more lucky ones will you encounter.

Summary: developing a business plan for raising money

Based on all the information that I have provided so far you should pick two to three strategies that you will apply.

In summary, I personally would recommend the following strategies:

1. Call center marketing team and follow up calls
2. Face-to-face meetings
3. Presentations

You should define clearly how much money you want to raise and what activities you will have to do on daily basis to accomplish your set targets.

Here is an example:

- Follow up calls (from leads that were generated by marketing cold calling call center) each day: 100 dials, 50 conversations, 20 good sales conversations
- Face-to-face meetings: Set 10 personal meetings each week—2 meetings each day—make 20 calls each day to set 2 new meetings
- Presentations: Organize 1 general presentation each month—invite 100 people to each presentation—20 people will actually show up

By breaking down your goals into daily activities you will always know what to do and if you are on track.

I strongly suggest that you make a written plan of action so that when emotions run low you know why you are doing the things that you are doing.

Prospect Memory Jogger

Here is a list to help you brainstorming:

The members of your own family

- Father and Mother
- Father-In-Law / Mother-In-Law
- Grandparents
- Children
- Brothers & Sisters
- Aunts and Uncles
- Nieces and Nephews
- Cousins

Those you meet in organizations or clubs

- Civic groups, Rotary, exchange, Jaycees
- Political clubs
- Lodge, Elks, Moose, Etc.
- Missionary societies, brotherhood groups
- Merchants or farm organizations
- School groups, boosters, alumni, PTA, etc.

List of acquaintances already available

- Christmas card list
- Address book
- Day timer, planner
- List of fellow employees
- Church directory

People who are decision makers

- Business owners
- Human Resources Directors
- Office managers

Those who are your closest friends with whom you associate regularly

- Friends and Neighbors
- People you work with
- Church members
- Sunday school class members

Those you have been associated with in the past

- Schoolmates
- Former co-workers
- People in your home town
- Military cohorts

Those you do business with

- Doctor, lawyer, barber, merchants, grocer
- Gas station attendant, dry cleaner, postal worker
- Beauticians, jewelers, waiters/waitresses

People you know who are in direct sales

- Business/office machine salespeople
- Insurance sales people
- Car salespeople

Do You Know Anyone Associated With Any of the Following Areas?

Accounting	Boys Clubs	Fishermen
Acting	Broadcasting	Florists
Advertising	Brokers	Food Service
Aerobics	Builders	Furniture
Air Force	Buses	Gardens
Airline	Cable TV	Gift Shops
Alarm Systems	Cameras	Girls Clubs
Animal Health/Vet	Camping	Golfing
Antiques	Crafts	Government
Apartment	Credit Union	Graphic Arts
Architect	Day Care	Grocery Stores
Army	Delivery	Gymnastics
Art	Dentists	Hair Care
Artificial Nails	Dermatologists	Handicapped
Asphalt	Designers	Handyman
Athletics	Detectives	Hardware
Auctioneer	Diet Industry	Health Clubs
Automobile	Direct Mail	Health Insurance
Baby-Sitters	Disk Jockey	Hearing Aids
Banking	Doctors	Helicopters
Barber	Driving Range	Hiking
Baseball	Dry Cleaners	Horses
Basketball	Dry Wall	Hospitals
Beauty salon	Education	Hotels
Beepers	Electrician	Hunting
Bible School	Engineering	Ice Cream
Bicycles	Entertainment	Ice Skating
Blinds	Eye Care	Income Tax
Boats	Fax Equipment	Insurance
Bond/Stocks	Farming	Investments
Books	Film Industry	Janitor
Bookkeeping	Firemen	Jewelry

Judo	Optometrists	Religion
Karate	Orthodontist	Rental agencies
Kindergarten	Painting	Reporters
Laundries	Parking	Resorts
Lawn Care	Parties	Rest Homes
Leather	Pediatricians	Restaurants
Leasing	Pedicures	Roller Blading
Libraries	Pensions	Roofing
Lighting	Perfume	Safety
Livestock	Personnel	Sales
Loans	Pest Control	Salons
Luggage	Pets	Sandblasting
Lumber	Pharmacies	Satellites
Mail	Phones	School
Management	Photography	Screen Printing
Manufacturing	Physician	Scuba Diving
Mathematics	Pianos	Secretaries
Mechanics	Pizza	Security
Mental Health	Plastics	Self Defense
Miniature Golf	Plumbing	Sewing Sheetrock
Mobile homes	Podiatrist	Shoe repair
Mortgages	Police	Siding
Motels	Pollution	Signs
Motion Pictures	Pools	Singing
Movie Theatres	Preschools	Skating
Museums	Printing	Skeet Shooting
Music	Property Mgmt.	Skiing
Mutual funds	Psychiatrists	Skin Care
Navy	Psychologists	Soccer
Newspapers	Publishers	Social Services
Nurses	Racing	Softball
Nutrition	Radio	Software
Office Machines	Railroad	Spas
Office Furniture	Real Estate	Sporting goods
Oil Changes	Rehabilitation	Steam cleaning

Stereos

Stocks

Surgeons

Surveyors

T-Shirts

Tailors

Tanning

Taxes

Teachers

Telecommunications

Telemarketing

Television

Tennis

Theatres

Therapists

Tile Layers

Tires

Title Companies

Tools

Towing

Townhouses

Training

Transmissions

Trucking

Typesetting

Unions

Universities

Upholstery

Used Cars

Vacuum Cleaners

Vending

Veterans

Video

Volunteers

Wallpaper

Waste

Watches

Water Skiing

Weddings

Wine

Woodworking

Writing

Zoos

Sales Psychology for Private Equity

Introduction to sales and communication

This sales training program is not based on theory. It is practical knowledge that has been used in over 3000 face-to-face meetings and thousands of phone calls.

Sales is the foundation for every business success

74% of all self-made millionaires are directly involved in the sales process of their products. Learn everything about sales there is to know. It is the foundation of every business transaction.

You need to understand human psychology so that you can position your products in the best possible way. You need to become a specialist in human behavior and develop your communicative abilities.

Some people believe that you need to be born as a sales person. That is true: you need to be born first in order to become a sales person. This is good news because sales ability is a skill that can be learned. It is not something that you either have or don't have. It is a series of techniques that can be learned and developed.

Everybody wants to be successful. It is not intelligence or knowledge that determines success. It is the ability of how someone can sell his ideas, products or himself.

There are a lot of sales people that earn more than a million dollars per year. This is not something that happens from one day to the next. It is a process and a development that someone had to go through. By improving each sales skill on a daily basis, you will get better and improve your results.

Why are some people more successful than others? It has to do with the law of cause and effect. Everything happens for a reason. Success and failure are both results of a specific cause that proceeded. If you want to have what other successful people have, then you must do the same things that they have done. And what others have done or achieved before you, you can do as well. You don't need to reinvent the wheel. You need to learn and copy those things that have made other sales people successful and you will be successful as well.

My story

Why am I qualified to talk about sales? Here is a quick look at my story:

At the age of 20 I got into straight commission sales. At the age of 21 I was earning $10,000 a month. By the time I was 23, I became the number one sales team leader in our company in Europe. There were 1000 other team leaders that I had to compete against. By that time I had hired and trained over 75 sales people. In the six years I was with this financial planning company I have had over 3000 face-to-face meetings with clients. Eventually, I got so good at my job that I had a perfect closing rate for over nine months. Usually, my closing rate was somewhere between 80 and 90%. During that time my team and I had raised over $400 million in financial and insurance products.

I taught other sales people how to become better in sales. I taught them topics like sales techniques, communication, financial consulting and financial basics.

Later, I was working for the largest independent hedge fund company in the world and with my sales team we raised over $245 million in four months. We raised the money from financial professionals, banks and institutional clients.

Later, I built my own companies and raised over $40 million for them though Private Equity. I had several sales organizations and over 60 people working for me.

This is not to brag but to show you that I have a lot of sales experience that you can benefit from.

Basics about communication

> Think like a wise man but communicate
> in the language of the people.
> (William Butler Yeats)

There are always four factors that need to be followed in order to make a sale. The first factor is likeability. No one will ever buy from you if they don't like you. In order for someone to like you, you need to make sure that you are smiling, are open and positive and that you have a welcoming and warm attitude or aura. Usually, you can develop likeability during small talk. Don't get straight to the point. Make sure that you develop rapport and that the other person likes you first. Show honest interest in the other person and give praise and recognition where it is possible and appropriate. You cannot proceed before you have laid a foundation of mutual likeability. If you skip this step, you will not sell anything.

The second factor is trust. A person will not buy from you if he or she doesn't trust you. They might like you but if they don't trust you, you will not sell anything.

You can develop trust by making sure that the way you look is appropriate, how you choose your words, how competent you appear, by being referred by others, your educational level, your level of self-confidence and eye contact.

The problem is not necessarily what you do or say, it is the other person's sub-conscious that will determine whether or not they trust you. If the other person gets a bad feeling he or she will not trust you. When two people communicate with each other only 5% happens on a verbal level and the other 95% are non-verbal.

Imagine that each one of us carries a Neanderthal on our backs. The Neanderthal represents our sub-conscious. The Neanderthal is much bigger and stronger than we are and he decides in the end what happens. If you can't win the trust of the Neanderthal then you have lost.

The third factor is finding a need. It is possible that the other person likes you and that he or she trusts you but if they don't really have a need to do business with you, they will not buy from you, either.

It is possible that your product might be ok but if the other person doesn't see a good reason for him—or herself to buy this product, then you won't sell it.

In order for someone to see the need for a product, you need to show your client his or her deficit first. You need to make him or her aware of a deficit. That means that you need to explain or create awareness about the negative implications of not having or using your product.

You need to show your client that his current situation is not as ideal or at ease as he may think. Only if you create a deficit and make him aware that he has a problem, will you be able to sell something.

A good example is life insurance. Once the client is aware of the possible consequences that his death might have for his family, he will develop the need or desire to buy life insurance.

And the last factor is price. Only after you have made sure that someone likes you, trusts you and has a need, then you are allowed to talk about the price. Everything else will kill the sale.

So let's summarize: LTNP

> Likeability before Trust before Need before Price

The goal of a successful communication

There is also a rule that applies here:

> said ≠ heard ≠ understood
>
> understood ≠ agreed
>
> agreed ≠ ready to do
>
> ready to do ≠ stick with it

There can be a lot of misunderstandings when it comes to communication. If, for example, the wife tells her husband to take out the garbage, it does not guarantee that he will actually do it. Just because she has said it to him does not necessarily mean that he has heard or understood it. Even if he has understood it, it does not mean that he agrees. And even if he agrees, it does not mean that he is ready to do it now or to keep doing it.

In order to solve this dilemma you need to ask control questions. In sales or general communication you can never simply assume. You always need to get clarity. Only if you have clarity, you know where you are. Therefore, you need to clarify each step along the way by asking control questions.

Communication is everything!

It is not important how much you know but how you apply it. People who are good communicators will earn more money and will generally be more accepted than others.

Everything counts: your facial expressions, how you emphasize something, how you pronounce something, how fast you talk, how loud you talk and what words you use.

How you use your language can make a huge difference. Let's say you ask a client the following questions:

1. I have something very interesting for you where you can make a lot of money. Are you available tonight? Let's meet on 1200 Main Street.

You will have less success if you say the following:

2. Are you available tonight? Let's meet on 1200 Main Street—just across from the cemetery.

Or for example if a man says to a woman:

1. Every time I look into your eyes, time stands still.

or:

2. When I see your face, every clock stops working.

Sometimes by simply changing around words, it can mean something completely different and the result will be different. Two religious people who are heavy smokers can ask for permission the two following ways:

1. Am I permitted to smoke while I pray?
2. Am I permitted to pray while I smoke?

Even though both ask basically the same thing, the answer and the result will be different.

Another factor might be how you are dressed. If you are in a jump suit that is full of oil and you try to convince someone of the advantages of a financial product, the outfit does not match the content of your conversation. No matter how good or important your content might be.

The same is true for the location of your conversation. Sometimes you should not discuss things in the restroom.

20 things to consider when dealing with clients

1. Always be honest. Avoid empty promises and half-truths. Be honest when it comes to negative aspects of your product in the beginning. This will actually build trust and credibility.
2. Don't hide behind your company's name. In the end it all depends on you as a person.
3. Tell clients more of those things that they want to hear.
4. Repeat the client's name often.
5. Don't be too pushy with clients. But make sure that you don't give up too easily when the client says "no" at first.

6. Build up curiosity. Don't tell the client everything right from the start. Make him curious so that he wants to know more.
7. Don't be afraid to ask questions. It is not the question but the way you ask for it.
8. Be excited and enthusiastic about your product.
9. The client should become your friend. Make sure he really likes you and that you like him.
10. Act with confidence when it comes to closing the sale.
11. Consult the client as if he were your brother.
12. Do more than is expected of you.
13. Know your products inside out.
14. Communicate clearly and in such a way that a ten year old will understand it.
15. Always show respect.
16. Always do things that increase the level of trust.
17. Create a win-win situation.
18. Make sure that your appearance is always as good as possible.
19. Don't treat everybody the same. Differentiate the types of clients and act accordingly.
20. Give lots of praise and recognition. This is something that everybody craves.

Question techniques

> Don't ask a woman if you can kiss her. Either do it or don't do it. But for God's sake don't ever ask a woman!
> (Umberto Saxer, sales trainer)

In every other case make sure you ask questions.

People who ask questions control the conversation. Make sure that you only talk 30% of the time and that your client talks 70% of the time. By asking questions you will be able to achieve that.

When you ask questions you will find out everything you need to know in order to make a sale.

Great sales people have all questions carefully prepared and thought through. They ask high quality questions that are emotional and that keep the client's attention. Never be afraid to ask personal questions. Always ask politely and positively.

The great thing about our society is that we are conditioned to answer questions when asked. Therefore, whoever asks a question, is leading the conversation.

Questions are a great way to extract information from a client. One technique is called the parrot technique. Like a parrot, you repeat the last word of a question that someone has asked you.

For example: If someone asks you if you are also dealing with derivatives but you have no idea what derivatives are, then you simply repeat the last word. You ask back: "Derivatives? What do you mean?" or "How do you mean?"

The client will then give you a more detailed form of his question. In that case you will gain time to consider your answer and be more accurate with it.

Types of questions

> You need to use sales techniques and rhetorical questions in such a way that the client doesn't realize that you are using a technique.

Closed questions

Closed questions always have a "yes" or "no" answer. It is either something positive or negative. For example: "Is your last name Smith?" or "Are you going to the movies tonight?"

You should try to avoid closed questions in a sales presentation. You might get the wrong answer and kill the sale.

Open questions

Open questions are typically questions that start with "how", "what", "who", "where" or "why". These types of questions will give you lots of information about the client or his circumstances. Examples are: "How did you get here today?" (The bus) or "What did you do after you got up this morning?" (Brushed teeth and had a shower)

Ask lots of open questions to find out more about the client.

Questions with options

These types of questions always offer a choice between two options. Often you need to help a client to make a decision. Instead of asking him a closed question by saying something like "would you like to do this deal?" you rather give him two options. Ask: "Would you prefer investing $20,000 or $30,000 into this product?" You never give him the option to say "no". His thoughts now focus on those two amounts and not whether he would like to do the deal or not.

Hypothetical questions

These types of questions open up the client for new ideas and possibilities. Some of those questions are: "Assuming you had a million dollars, what would you do with it?" or "Imagine there was no more Coca Cola, what would that mean for the world?" or "Would it not be better if we all had a better sleep?"

You can use these kinds of questions with closed up clients that initially don't show any interest in your products. You could ask: "Provided I was able to show you a way how to double your money in twelve months, would you give me five minutes of your time?"

Rhetorical questions

Rhetorical questions are questions where is answer is already clear from the beginning. Examples are: "Your name is Smith, isn't it?" or "You want to pay less taxes, don't you?" or "You wouldn't like it if someone hit you on the head, right?"

These questions can be quite direct and attacking. You need to get a good feeling for when you can use them and when to let it be.

Suggestive questions

In this case you try to imply something into your client. These kinds of questions target things like honor, community, status or image. If you found out that this is something that is important to your client, then you can use that kind of question.

Examples: "I am sure that an intelligent person like yourself doesn't like to see a situation like that, right?" or "You definitely want to do something against those ever raising taxes, don't you?'

Control questions

Control questions help you to make sure that your client has really understood all the things that you have mentioned during a presentation. If you just keep a monolog and never ask any control questions, you might risk losing the client somewhere along the way. That is why you need to frequently ask a control question to make sure every important topic or point has been understood and agreed upon.

Examples: "Was this point clear so far?" or "Did you understand the importance of this point?" or "Has everything made sense so far?"

<u>Counter questions</u>
These types of questions will buy you time and give you more information before you have to give an answer back. Examples are: "How do you mean?" or "What exactly do you mean by ... ?" The parrot technique is also a counter question technique.

Praise and recognition

> There are only two things that people
> want more than sex and money:
> Praise and recognition!
> (Mary Kay Ash)

Most people don't get enough praise and recognition in life. Make sure you give out lots and lots of praise when dealing with your clients. You will win a lot of people this way.

A typical response should always start with praise. If someone asks you a question, you should always start with some of these expressions:

"That is an interesting question."
"Thank you very much for mentioning this."
"It's great that you mention that. Most people would never do that."

After that you should use an expression of understanding. This can be something like this:

"I can really understand this."

"I feel the same."

"I appreciate your honesty with me."

"I am not surprised that someone like you has so little time."

"I am sorry to hear that."

"I really feel for you."

And finally you ask a question back.

The formula is:

---

1. Praise and recognition
2. Expression of understanding
3. New question

Example:

Client: "This product seems too expensive!"

Answer: "Thank you very much for mentioning that. I think it's great that you are so straightforward with me. Most people wouldn't do that. (Praise and recognition) I am not surprised that you feel that this product seems expensive at first. (Expression of understanding) Assuming I was able to show you a product that offers a lot of advantages that others don't have, even though it was a bit more expensive, would you generally be open to have a look at it?" (New question)

Dealing with a conflict

If you try to win an argument with a client you can only lose. Don't try to convince your client by confronting him directly with your sales arguments.

In a situation like that you need to first open up your client to your ideas by using the techniques that we just covered (praise and recognition, etc.)

If a client says: "I don't need your product!" you could reply like this:

"I am glad that you tell me this so directly. If I was in your shoes I would probably react exactly the same way." (Praise and recognition, expression of understanding)

By giving this answer you move your client from a negative to a more neutral point of view.

You continue: "Let me make the following suggestion: Assuming I knew something that would give you a tremendous financial advantage that you didn't know yet, wouldn't it make sense to spend at least five minutes on this topic? After you have had a chance to look at it, you can still decide whether or not this is right for you, agreed?"

Practice makes perfect

Even though some of those types of questions seem complicated at first, it is important to practice them so that they become natural. Eventually, people will not realize that you are using a technique. So make sure you practice these techniques with your friends or your sales coach. It will make a big difference in your sales results!

Prospecting

> The main reason why some people don't like to do prospecting is not necessarily to fear of rejection. The main reason is that they are simply not good at prospecting. Therefore decide to become the best at prospecting.
> (Brian Tracy)

General points

If you are doing no prospecting and suddenly switching to a lot of prospecting can be overwhelming. An easy to understand analogy is to imagine that you have never run in the past and you are going to take up running to get yourself into shape. Depending on your current physical condition, you start out with only a quarter mile. Eventually, you will be running longer distances.

Prospecting has a very predictable result. If you put more effort into the process, you will achieve a greater result. However, your success will never be immediate. Depending on the life cycle of the selling process, it may take a few weeks until you can see some results.

If you make 5 calls a day that equals 25 calls a week. If you have 50 work weeks x 25 calls a week you end up with 1250 calls a year. Do you think you would sell more if you did an extra 1250 calls a year?

Prospecting must be part of your daily activities, no matter what. If you are not successful at prospecting, it's unlikely you will be a successful salesperson.

Remember that your database is your most valuable asset. It is important to have a system that will allow you keep track of all your prospects. Sales is always a numbers game. When you make 100 calls you will always have a result. For example:

100	Dials
50	Completed calls
13	Appointments
13	Proposals
5	Sales
$	20,000

(Dials: the number of times you pick up the phone and press the number on your phone and it starts ringing. This also includes getting voice mail or the person's assistant.
Completed calls: This is when you actually reach the person intended and talk to him.)

In our case you could apply numbers like this and then predict your sales result:

100 completed calls
10 information packages
1 client
$ 20,000 average investment

10 clients = $200,000 in raised capital

Most sales people are afraid of rejection. Most people try to avoid doing prospecting by procrastinating or doing endless research before they call up anybody. The trick is to alter your perceptions of prospecting and rejection.

If your prospects would know exactly what you know about the product, they would buy it. Your job is to explain to them what you know. A "no" is never final. Sometimes the time is simply not yet right for the client to do business with you. But that doesn't mean that they won't do business with you in the future.

You cannot lose a game when you control when it ends. You cannot lose what you never had.

Preparation

- Create a positive atmosphere
- Put away everything from your desk except your calling list
- Have your appointment schedule ready

Set goals

- How many people do I want to talk to?
- What is the objective of each call? Sending out information or getting a meeting?
- How many meetings do I want to get?

Handling

- Watch your body posture. Sit straight or stand up.
- Keep the phone in front of your mouth. Make sure it is not on your neck.
- Remember that the most important thing is the client likes you at first. Therefore smile!
- Adjust your voice to the other person.
- Don't forget to pause on the right moments.

Mental attitude

It is normal that people will say "no" at first. Never take it personally! Remember that there is always a certain percentage of people who will buy your product in the end. The goal is simply to improve the number of people that will buy from you.

If, for example, it is your goal to get five appointments out of the 25 people that you call, then every "no" will bring you a step closer to your "yeses". Keep a positive attitude until you have completed your 25 calls.

Remember also the benefits of the product that you are selling. You are helping your clients to do better.

If you are in a bad mood, you should take a break. Your client can feel if you are not happy or motivated on the other side of the line. Only make phone calls with a happy, energetic and positive attitude. Only then will you succeed.

You can also motivate yourself the following way: Let's say you want to earn $10,000 a month. If $10,000 equals 6% in commission, then you would have to raise $166,000. In order to raise $166,000 you will need ten clients (if your average investment is somewhere between $15,000 and $20,000 per client). In order to get ten clients, you need to have send out 100 documentations. In order to send out 100 documentations, you will need to make 1000 calls. If you divide now $10,000 by 1000 calls, then you will realize that you make $10 per call—no matter what the outcome!

Create curiosity

> There is only one animal in the world that is
> more curious than the cat: the human!

Think about how you can incorporate curiosity into your sales process. You could ask the following questions:

"What would it mean to you if you had all of a sudden more money?'

"Assuming I was able to show you a way to save more taxes, would that be of interest to you?"

"Let's open up an account, put zero dollars into it and after five years you will have $13,000. Would you like to know how that works? Well then let's schedule an appointment."

It is ok to be provocative in certain situations.

What is the main objective of your call?

The main objective is either to send out the information package or to get an appointment—nothing else. Don't try to convince your client or sell anything in the first call.

Typical call structure

1. Introduction
2. Reason for calling
3. Introduction of your services
4. Create curiosity
5. Make a proposal

Reason for calling

"My name is Norman Meier. Does that ring any bells yet? No? Well then let me introduce myself."

"My name is Norman Meier. You probably have already heard my name. No? Well then let me introduce myself."

"We have a mutual friend: Mr. Smith. He told me to give you a call and give you his regards."—Thank you!

"Just the other day I was able to show him a great investment opportunity. He told me that I absolutely had to call you as well and let you know about it. He was very excited about the opportunity."

Important points

- Create positive mood! Nothing is more important than to have a positive conversation.
- Let the prospect know that there is no obligation.
- Try to get a lot of "yeses".
- It is normal for people to be skeptical at first. Don't let that discourage you.
- Write down the most common objections and create good answers.

Handling objections on the phone

"I am not interested!"

Real translation: The client doesn't yet know what you know. You either haven't created enough curiosity or he is still afraid. Give him time and don't push him. Suggest that he should first look at the marketing material and then he can still decide whether or not he wants to invest.

"I can understand that at this point you are not interested. That is totally normal. This is because you don't know yet exactly what I have to offer. Let me make a suggestion: why don't we have a short meeting and I can explain to you a little bit in detail and with documents what I mean exactly and then you can still decide whether or not this is of interest to you. Is that a fair suggestion?"

"I can understand how you must feel. I am calling you out of the blue and you think that I am just trying to sell you something. But that is not the case. I am a financial professional and I have helped a lot of people to improve their financial situation. Most people react with skepticism at first but after they get to know me, they don't regret having dealt with me. So let me make a suggestion: In order for you to get a feeling of whether or not I am worth spending some time with, I will send you some information about a product that will go public next year. It is extremely hot right now and the offer is very attractive. Why don't you have a look at the info that I am going to send you and I will give you a call in a few days to answer any questions you might have? Is that a fair proposal?"

"I have no money!"

Two options: Either the client really has no money or he is afraid. The level of trust at this point is still very weak. It is possible that the prospect doesn't see a need at this point in time. Don't try to argue with the prospect. Ask him some questions to find out more about his situation.

"Thank you for being so honest with me. Let me make the following suggestion . . ."

"I have no time!"

Real translation: He doesn't want to be bothered and lose time because he doesn't see the benefit at this point in time.

Answer: "I am not surprised that someone like you is very busy and has very little time. Because of that you will only take time out of your busy schedule if it is really something worthwhile, correct?"

"Correct!"

"In that case I assume that you would only be interested in a very short conversation, am I right?"

"Right!"

"Well then I suggest that we only meet for 15 minutes and I show you exactly what I have to offer. After that you can still decide whether or not you want to invest more time into that, agreed?"

"Agreed!"

"What it is and how does it work exactly?"

Note: If you give him any kind of information at this point in time, you will kill the sale. The question shows that he is curious but your objective is to get the meeting.

Answer: "Your question shows me that you seem very interested in getting further information. It would make more sense if we meet for a short 15 minutes and I can explain to you in detail what this is all about. When is it most convenient for you next week?"

"I lost money before!"

Real translation: This means that he is afraid to make another mistake. In that case you need to be careful and try to build up trust. You could mention things like the size of your company, reputation and so on. You won't be able to convince him in the first meeting to buy your product. Ideally, you need to set up a personal meeting.

Answer: "I am sorry to hear that. I am sure your advisor back then did not do it on purpose and he must not have done his due diligence properly. In our case the situation is a lot different. We have raised over $200 million from private investors in the last ten years and not in a single case did we get a complaint or lawsuit of any kind. You can imagine that we must deal with a lot of clients and that we make sure that the products that we offer are extremely well analyzed and selected.

In order for you to get a better idea of what it is that we do and what we offer I would suggest that we have a short meeting and I can explain to you how it works exactly. Does that sound fair?"

"My friend already works as a broker!"

Answer: "I am not surprised that you already know a broker. Most of my clients have really good brokers already. Please understand that I don't want you to change brokers. You can still continue to work with him and keep your assets there. The difference is that I have something to offer that he cannot offer. Our company specializes in pre-IPO financings and the deals that we take public are exclusively offered through our company. Can I make the following suggestion: Why don't I send you some basic information about a current deal that we are taking public and you can have a look at it. Does that sound fair?"

Dealing with objections

> Most people don't want to buy anything at first!

When you get an objection it is important to stay calm and positive. Getting an objection is normal and you should expect it. Basically, an objection is nothing else than a question. A client is still unsure and needs more information. If he doesn't object, then he has no interest. Therefore, an objection is a positive thing. Be happy to get an objection. Welcome it positively and your client will be surprisingly open for your answer.

When you get an objection, read between the lines. What does it really mean? If he says he has no money it does not necessarily mean that he has zero dollars. It could mean that he is afraid of losing money, he doesn't trust you or that he doesn't think that his savings of $200,000 would qualify him to be an investor. You need to find out the real reason behind an objection.

Prepare all possible objections in advance. Write them down and create answers. The more possible arguments you have the more calm will you be.

Put yourself into your client's shoes. Empathize with him and try to feel where he is at emotionally. Show understanding for his situation and think about how you could move him into the right direction.

Studies have shown that sales people who doubt their own products have gotten more objections using the same script as sales people who believe in their products. The only difference is their mental attitude.

Cold calling script example

Mr. Jones, please.

Hello, Mr. Jones.

This is Norman Meier of ABC Financial Services. How are you today?

Great!

We have not spoken before, . . .

   a) *. . . but a mutual friend of ours, Mr. Smith, has referred you.*
   b) *. . . and I would like to introduce myself.*

I work for a stock brokerage firm who specializes in the pre-IPO financing business of start-up companies. We finance companies that will go public and give investors a chance to participate in attractive private placements of promising stocks.
Our company has been around for ten years and we have raised over $200 million for all kinds of private equity deals.

Are you currently investing into the market?

   a) *Currently, we have a very attractive new deal that will go public at the end of 2011 at $0.50 and we are offering the shares for $0.25 right now. The company that we are taking public is in the resource sector and has projects that have already proven gold reserves.*
   b) *Currently, we have a very interesting and great new deal that will go public, soon. I am not sure if you are aware that there is usually a very high return potential when you get into a stock before it is public.*

In order to give you a more detailed overview what this deal is all about, I would like to send you some general information about the company so that you will understand what this is all about. Does that sound fair?

Great! Then I am happy to send you the info. What is your email address?
I will give you a call again in a few days so that we can discuss what I have just sent you.

Have a nice day!

First meeting with a client

The goal of the first meeting is not to make a sale. The main goal is to gather information and to pre-sell, so that you can use all the information that you get in the first meeting, to make a sale in the second meeting. Usually, a financial advisor needs to take all the information of a person into consideration, make a financial analysis or plan and then present the client with solutions. You should ask lots of questions and find out what the clients really wants.

Overview

- Introduction and talk about referrals
- Green round (small talk and improving likability)
- Referral deal
- Presentation with laptop
- Questionnaire
- Pre-closing questions
- Referral sheet and deal
- Make appointment for next week

Introduction and talk about referrals

Thanks for meeting with me here today.

Let me first introduce myself. I am a licensed stockbroker with FINRA. I specialize in Private Equity. We mainly focus on accredited investors. Those are people with at least $200,000 in personal income, $300,000 in household income or one million in net worth.

As you know, Larry Smith, a friend of yours, referred me to you. Did he say anything about his meetings with me?

Anyway, I just wanted to let you know that this is how we conduct our business. We are in a highly specialized field and we bring a great deal of financial advantages to our clients. That is why I don't just call anybody and annoy people by doing cold calls. I work strictly with referrals. That means that if someone was happy with my advice and what I had to show him, I always get referrals from my clients. That is the most professional way of doing business because we have to select the type of clients very carefully. And that is how I got here with you today, as well.

(The main goal is to create a logical "bridge" to getting referrals later. Also, you need to position yourself, as an absolute expert and that he can be happy that you took your time to be there in the first place. You are not a sales person who is bothering a client with a sales offer. You are a specialist just like a doctor or lawyer.)

Green round

- So how long have you known Larry?
- Do you work together or are you just friends?

- Tell me about yourself.
- Are you currently investing into the market?
- How is that working out for you so far?

Referral deal

Now, before we begin, I would like to make a deal with you.

What I am about to show you can dramatically increase your financial performance. I am going to do a short presentation about what it is that we do and what we have to offer exactly.

Question 1: Assuming you really like what I have to offer, would you be willing to refer me to other people—just like I came here through Larry?

The answer has to be a clear "yes". If the answer is fuzzy, repeat the question or say:

But let's say that you really, really like it and you would be really excited about our products, would you be willing to give me referrals of your friends and contacts?

Question 2: Usually, I get between 20 and 30 referrals from my clients. Can we do the same?

The answer should also be a clear "yes". If he says "yes", say: "thank you" and shake his hand. This will seal the deal.

Great, then I will now show you what I have to offer.

If he says: "What! That amount is way too much!"

Your reply should be: Yes. 20 to 30 names! Everybody knows about 200 people in their inner circle and even up to a 1000 people in the outer circle. That is way too much. All I want is 20 to 30 names. Can we please do the same? I will help you with it, ok?

Presentation

I am going to show you a short presentation on my laptop so that you understand what I have to offer and then I am going to ask you a few questions about your current situation. Let's get started!

So, what is Private Equity and how does it work?

When a company is listed on a stock exchange, it is considered to be a public company. When it is not yet listed, it is called a private company. The term "Equity" simply refers to stocks.

In the long run, stocks usually out perform any other asset classes and smaller companies can develop much more in value in the beginning. A big company like McDonald's is unlikely to double in price within one year but a small start-up company can double, triple or grow even further.

When looking at a stock chart, it is only possible to see the first price when the company was first listed. The company however has been around for a longer period of time and usually got financed through private financings. These financing rounds are called private placements. If a company does a first round of financing at for example $0.40 a share, it might raise capital for future business development. The company might continue to raise capital by using several financing rounds before it goes public. These rounds may be at the $0.50, $0.65 or the $0.80 level. The general public will then only be able to buy stocks when the company is listed at $1.00 for example. But investors, who were able to buy the stocks for $0.40 per share, have already more than doubled their money.

PRE-CLOSING QUESTIONS:

1. Imagine you were able to get into a project at the $0.40 level and you could get out at around a dollar. What would you think about that?
2. Do you think that would be a great opportunity?
3. What if I had something similar like that to show you, would you be interested in looking at it?
4. What if I brought you an investment opportunity like that, would you consider investing into it?
5. Great, then I will show you something next time.

The advantages of Private Equity are that there are no price fluctuations, are able to participate in the beginning of a new venture when the price of a share is at its cheapest, have a high return on investment potential and a relatively short investment horizon of only 6 to 24 months.

We are offering shares to accredited (or wealthy) private investors of companies that are not yet listed or trading. The transaction is called Private Placement and is an offer to purchase shares of private companies. The plan is to finance companies that will eventually go public in a stock market (IPO = Initial public offering). We are offering our investors attractive investment possibilities with a chance of getting high returns.

Not every Private Equity deal is a success. It is possible that some deals fail but others go through the roof. That is why it is wise to invest into a series of different projects to spread the risk and get a diversification of the portfolio.

Private Equity is considered a high-risk type of investment. This is the case because new companies have a higher risk to go bankrupt. In fact 85% of new companies fail in the first three years. The main reasons are 1. Lack of capital, 2. Poor management and 3. Bad products with no market.

This is where ABC Capital provides value. We provide the financing for companies by raising money from investors. Our team of brokers will raise money as a combined force and therefore ensure that companies get properly financed.

We build the share structure for companies that will enable us to take it public, put in experienced management and only chose products that we believe to be a great success in the market.

For example, if we simply gave $5 million to a scientist who invented a great product, it is not ensured that the company will be successful. The scientist may be great in his area of expertise but he may simply lack management skills, financial knowledge, marketing skills, etc. and may not know how to make a company successful in the stock market.

Therefore, we keep a close control over the company in the beginning to ensure that it goes into the right direction. By doing so, we protect the interests of our investors until they have an exit.

We invest in a variety of industries. Mainly we focus on resources, biotechnology, life science, real estate or technology projects. The decision to finance a particular project is dependent on several factors and we are open to most industries.

When we are putting together a new project, a series of factors need to be considered: the shell (corporation), management team, financing, specialist team (e.g. geological team), projects or products, legal counsel, administrational support, accounting, financial knowledge, investor relations, contact of networks, strategic action plan and exit for investors.

When we are considering a new project, we need to determine whether the project will be a success in the future. We have to decide if the company's products or services will actually be marketable, what the quality standards are, if distribution channels need to be established, what the financing requirements will be and if the stock will have sufficient trading volume in the market. Only if all these factors can be answered positively, we are willing to finance a new project.

PRE-CLOSING QUESTIONS:

1. Assuming I was able to show you a project that was structured exactly the way I just described would you be interested in looking at it?
2. Normally, it is possible to calculate the stock price of a project when it is public. Now, imagine if I were able to show you a project that is about to go public with a clear valuation of let's say a dollar and you would be able to get in at a level of about 10 to 25% of the current value. How great would that be?

Questionnaire

Well, before I can show you something like that, I need to ask you a few questions to determine if what exactly I can show you and if you qualify.

PRE-CLOSING QUESTIONS:
Goals

1. What are your goals and objectives?

2. Let's see how we can achieve these goals with Private Equity. What if I were able to show you something next time we meet that would bring you closer to your dreams and goals, would you be interested in that?
3. Would you take advantage of that if you like it?

Risk tolerance

Let's see how your risk profile looks like. Based on your risk profile we can decide how much we can allocate into Private Equity.

Investor profile

1. Based on this summary, I would say that you are a ... investor. In this case you should allocate at least ... % into Private Equity.

Basic Asset Allocation

Studies from Yale and Notre Dame suggest that you invest a substantial amount of your portfolio into Private Equity.

1. Of your total net worth how much do you have allocated into Private Equity today?
2. Based on the analysis how much should you be investing into Private Equity?

Private Equity process and financing rounds

Remember this slide? It shows again the process of the timing and how beneficial it is to invest as early as possible.

Based on your assets what amount would you be able to invest?

If I were able to find an appropriate Private Equity investment for you, would you be Interested in looking at it?

If I were able to show you the benefits of this investment, would you be willing to invest?

<u>Assets and cash liquidity</u>

As a general rule of thumb, you should only have two to three months of cash liquid. This is to pay your bills and to pay for any unexpected things. The rest should be invested otherwise you lose money because of inflation like I showed you earlier in the presentation.

I can see that you have a lot of . . .
I would suggest switching a few things around and making sure that you allocate about 10% into Private Equity. The rest could be invested into . . .

When I look at your current investments and how much cash you have, this would be about $50,000.

If I can show you a Private Equity investment opportunity for $50,000 that would bring you all the advantages and benefits that we just talked about, would you be interested in looking at it?

What if you really, really like it, would you take advantage of my offer?

Great, then I will do my best to find you a suitable opportunity for when we meet next week.

Referral sheet and deal

Did you like what I had to show you today so far?
Do you think that Private Equity is a great investment opportunity?
Do you think that others could benefit from this as well?
Do you remember what we talked about in the beginning?

I would like to make a deal with you. I am going to show you a project that will fulfill exactly your needs and will be an opportunity to make a lot of money for you. That is my job. And your job is to fill out the form with names. Agreed?

Great! Then I will do my best to earn those referrals next time.

Second meeting

After the first meeting you scheduled a second meeting with the client to discuss your findings. The goal of this meeting is to make a sale.

Overview

- Goals and dreams

Let's look at the goals and dreams that you have selected last time. You told me that you wanted to

1. Build wealth
2. Improve investment performance
3. Save money for retirement

Is that still the case?

You also told me that you want to buy a boat in the next five years. (Mention a dream that he has told you in the first meeting) Do you still want to boat? Your dream boat costs about $300,000. What if I had a strategy to be able to get you that boat, would you like that? Great, then let's make it a reality.

Based on your investor profile and your investment experience, you should be able to invest about 10% into Private Equity. Based on your assets, that equals about $50,000.

In our last meeting you told me that you would be interested in an investment opportunity for that amount. Is that still the case or has something changed since last week?

Great, then I will show you how to achieve these goals.

But before we begin, did you remember our deal from last time? Great, then I will do my best to earn this list.

I want to start again with the basic modules about Private Equity that we have talked about and what their great advantages are.

Ask control questions like:

1. By investing before a company goes public what advantages do you have?
2. By getting in early, what is your potential?
3. Does this strategy make sense?
4. Is everything I explained so far clear?

Show presentation about gold and XYZ CORP

CLOSING:

Let's go back to your goals and dreams and let's see what we can check off with this investment, shall we?

Check off each point.

Wow, with XYZ CORP we are able to achieve all your goals and dreams. Isn't that amazing?

There is only one thing: We are ten brokers working on this financing right now and it is extremely hot and popular. I can't guarantee that this investment will be around for very long because it is only $2.5 million. It is possible that just in a few days the financing will be closed or oversubscribed. Therefore, you should act now. I have double checked with my boss and made a reservation for the $50,000 for you.

In order to secure this deal, the next step is simply to fill out this share subscription agreement right here. Shall I fill it out or do you want to fill it out?

Objection:

I still need to think about it!

Oh, I am sorry. What exactly did I not explain clearly? What exactly do you need to think about?

I am not sure about the risk involved.

Ok, let's look at that again. Anything else?

What about the IPO: How do I know that the company really goes public?

Anything else?

What about the management team? Can they really pull it off?

Anything else?

No, that's all.

Ok. If I can answer these three points to your satisfaction, would you invest then?

Yes.

Ok then let's go through it.

Check off each point.

Second telephone conversation after initial IP

- Hi (Name). This is John from ABC Capital. We spoke a couple of days ago and I sent you some information. How are you today?
- Did you have a chance to look at the material that I have sent you?
- No? That's ok. Let me just give you the five minute overview.
- As you might remember, we are a licensed stockbrokerage firm specialized in Private Equity projects. The main advantage of Private Equity is that you can invest into a stock before it goes public at the lowest price possible and get great returns.
- Typically, people invest at, for example, $0.50 per share and when the company goes public it is at a dollar. From

there the stock depending on the company can go up to several dollars.

- I have sent you a project that is in the gold sector and it is called XYZ CORP. Have you followed gold lately? No? Yes? (Doesn't matter)—Just 10 years ago gold was at $300 per ounce and now it is over $1500. Many experts predict gold to be in the $2000 to $3000 range. So the timing for gold investments couldn't be better.

- XYZ CORP is an amazing deal. The company has all the factors to become a superstar in the gold business.

- Typically, gold exploration companies are looking for gold deposits and if you are lucky the stock will go up. In XYZ CORP's case however, they have already found 500,000 ounces of gold and therefore the company has virtually no risk in regards to whether or not there is gold in the first place.

- Having said that, at gold prices of $1500 per ounce, you can only take $100 per ounce of gold in the ground. In this case if you multiply 500,000 with $100 you will get a valuation of $50 million.

- The company will have 25 million shares outstanding and a fair share price should be at $2.00 per share.

- Currently, the company does a private placement for a limited amount of an amazing price of $0.25 per share. I can hardly believe it myself. This is the case because it's the company's first financing round and I know that in about one or two weeks they will increase the price significantly. So the time to take action is right now.

- Some people initially argue with me that because it is a new company, the deal is apparently more risky. That might seem the case at first but if you know that the management team has done similar deals just like this in the past, you will see that it is a no brainer.

- Tom Black, for example, was involved with ABC Resources that went from $0.70 a share to over $13. He was also ...

- The geological team is first class. The chief geologist, John White, was the chief geologist of the biggest Canadian gold mine in history.

- Those people have been in this business for over 20 years each at least and have proven track records.
- There are a few more reasons why this is a great investment. Actually, there are 10 reasons. Let me quickly summarize them.
- So, now let's talk a little bit about your situation. How was your recent performance in the stock market lately? Well, in that case, I think that XYZ CORP could make a nice little addition.
- When we look at your liquid assets, what range would be a possibility for you? $20,000 to $50,000, $50,000 to $100,000 or more than $100,000?
- $25,000? That's great. Why don't you give it a try?
- Possible questions or objections . . .
- Listen, this deal is extremely hot right now and I know that you will be happy with it. I would love to win you as a client.
- Why don't we start with this deal first and over the next few weeks and months I will be showing you a number of great opportunities and I will provide you with great investment tips. This deal is really at the lowest price possible and it might not be there next week. Therefore I suggest we act right now.
- I will send you the SSA right now. That is the contract. And then you can read it, fill it out, ask any questions you might have and let get started. I promise you that you will not regret it.

Sales process overview

Call

- Goal: set a meeting

1st meeting

- Build rapport

- Build trust
- Find out information about your client
- Find out about his goals and dreams (what does he want?)
- Do the presentation (only PE, ABC)
- Explain advantages of PE
- Do an analysis of his financial situation using a questionnaire
- Use modules
- Create curiosity
- Show him that he has a deficit and that you have a solution for his problems
- Ask pre-selling questions
- Determine how much money he has free to invest
- Determine his risk profile
- Determine whether or not he is an accredited investor or non-accredited investor
- Find out what industries he might like (resources, biotech, real estate, technology or other)
- Determine a specific amount that he could invest
- Find out if that money is available now or when it is available
- Set the second meeting

2nd meeting

- Develop a positive atmosphere
- Go through his goals and dreams again
- Ask if anything changed in the meantime
- Ask a pre-closing question about if he would invest today
- Do the presentation (about Private Equity, gold and XYZ CORP)
- Ask closing questions
- Close the deal
- Fill out the SSA (Share subscription agreement) together with him

Taking a prospect to the next level and turning it into a client

The time frame to close a deal can vary but it's typically anywhere from two to four weeks. In the first week an IP (information package) is being sent out, in the second week you need to follow up and in the third week you can close the deal. Between each step is a series of steps that you should consider.

Week 1   Sending out IP (Information package)
Week 2   Meeting / phone call to follow up / sending out more information
Week 3   Closing the deal

After you have sent out the initial IP you should follow up a few days after. The following scenarios can take place:

1.   The client has read the information
2.   The client has not read the information

The objective of the initial call is to be able to send out information to get the client curious. Whether or not the client has read the information, now the real selling process begins. You cannot assume that the potential client has understood the real value of the information that you have sent him. The main focus is now to explain the product and make the presentation.

If this process is done over the phone, you should schedule about fifteen to thirty minutes for a client.

You can say the following things:

- Dear Mr. Jones, I have sent you some information a few days ago. Where you able to review the information? No? That's ok, I am happy to explain the main features to you.

Yes? What did you find most interesting? I would like to point out a few interesting features about this product.

You need to have a clear objective of what the next step should be and you need to lead the conversation. You cannot just call and hope that it goes well. You should know exactly what it is that you want to talk about and what the next step should be BEFORE you make the call.

Objectives:

1. Send out more information
2. Schedule a personal meeting
3. Schedule a telephone meeting
4. Go through the material and explain the main features in a telephone conversation.
5. Get referrals

You should always know in advance what your objective is and then follow through.

You could, for example, talk about the product features and get him really interested. Talk about the main reasons why the investment is a good choice and then suggest sending out some more information. Then schedule a second telephone meeting where you know that the client has some time available.

In the second telephone meeting, you need to talk further about the positive aspects of this investment.

The main goal over all is to develop a relationship with the client and to find out those things that he is most interested in. Also, ask a lot of questions to find out what kind of potential the client has and how much experience in the stock market he has.

Closing phase

In rare cases you can close a client shortly after having sent out the IP. This is not the normal course of action because there is no trust level established. The only exception would be a client that has been referred and has a good relationship with another client who did the investment.

Typically, there is a series of closing questions that you need to ask.

The first objective is to explain to the client the product and then to ask a control question whether or not he has a good understanding of the product.

Then you should ask a qualifying question: "If you were to invest into this product, would you be able to invest anywhere from $20,000 to $50,000, $50,000 to $100,000 or more than $100,000? Where is your range?

You could get two kinds of answers:

1. He will give you a range.
2. He will give you resistance.

If he gives you a range, that is a good sign. You have to define a clear number and then you keep mentioning that number. The goal is to eliminate all the factors that are unclear. He might have a series of questions or concerns still at this point but if you have at least defined an amount, then you can focus on the remaining objections.

If he gives you resistance, then he is not yet ready for the closing phase. He might still have a lot of questions or is worried about the risk.

You can ask the following questions:

1. Now that I have given you a good overview what this product is all about, can you confirm that you understand the main features of this product? YES
2. We talked about the positive aspects and reasons why this would be a good investment. Would you generally agree? YES
3. You said that a possible investment could be $50,000. Is that a number that you would feel is comfortable to invest? YES
4. There is only one problem. (PAUSE) Client: What is it?— Broker: We don't have much time. It is very likely that the number of shares that I can give you, will be gone in a few days. Therefore, you need to act now. (MAKE IT RARE, TAKE IT AWAY, TIME PRESSURE)

If he has objections and you cannot go easily through the YES questions, you can do the following:

Mr. Jones, I see that you are still worried about a few things, right? YES
What exactly are the things that you still feel unsure about?

1. Risk
2. Validity
3. Stock price
4. Exit

Great. Anything else?

Yes, the geologist. What about it exactly?

Ok. Let's add the geologist as the fifth point to the list.

I can see that there are still a few things that we need to clear up. Now assuming that we can clear up all these five questions / concerns and you feel positive and comfortable about them, would you then do the investment? YES

Good, then let's look at the first point.

TALK ABOUT RISK AND ELIMINATE THE FEAR

Now after having just explained the first point. Do you think we can check it off? YES

Ok, let's look at concern number two . . .

Do this until all concerns are covered. Then go back to the closing questions and close the deal.

Why people buy Private Equity stocks

> Greed is the number one reason why people buy pre-IPO stocks

People always believe that there is something out there in the financial world that can make them rich overnight. Most people believe that there is a secret investment or strategy that is kept from the average person and if they only found a way to access this kind of investment, then they could become rich, too.

Of course, Private Equity deals can offer such a great investment but most of them are also very risky and losing money is more likely than hitting it big. Despite all the warnings in the contract, people still choose risk over security.

Getting the first investment from a client

The main goal is to get a client to buy any amount of shares at first. Even if the amount is only a few thousand dollars at first, it is important to get the client to invest. The reason for this is as follows: Once a client has said "yes" to the investment, he doesn't want to lose it anymore. He gave you his initial trust and he believes in the deal. Now, you have a reason to keep contacting your client for other deals or to increase the existing investment amount. This is called loading a client.

One client had initially invested $1700 and by looking at the client's profile you could think that he was a small fish. The first deal didn't work out and the sales person contacted the client again and explained to him why the first deal went bust. Then on the second deal, the client invested a $100,000 into a second deal and a month later another $200,000 into the same deal. Usually, loading clients is much more lucrative. There are sales people who specialize in opening clients (getting the initial investment) and sales people who specialize in loading clients. Those are two different approaches.

Negative selling

If an investor has already invested into your deal, he is like most people. He doesn't want to lose his investment. If the company is in trouble and you are trying to save it, you can always approach a client and tell him if he doesn't invest more money, the company and therefore his investment will be lost. By reinvesting another time he will secure his investment that he has already made. Sometimes this strategy is the only way to raise capital for a company that is going down and it is its only chance to recover. Unfortunately, a lot of mistakes have been made in a deal like that and the only people who can save it are the existing investors.

Unfortunately, dodgy sales people are abusing negative selling techniques. Sometimes it is better to call it quits than to make matters worse.

Sales techniques and dealing with objections of investors

Typical sales process

1. Cold calling—Lead Generation (first call)
2. Follow up call (general information, explanation and creating interest)
3. Sales call and contract
4. Dealing with objections and questions
5. Closing the deal
6. Loading the client

Understanding the psychology of objections

Objections are normal. Nobody wants to buy a product at first. If you don't get objections, then there is no interest. Objections are nothing else but questions. If you get objections, then you should welcome them with open arms. They are buying signals.

Techniques and phrases

The following is a summary of different sales techniques and phrases that can be used when dealing with investors. The idea is to close the deal and get them to act. Of course, there is always a certain amount of time that has proceeded in order to build trust and to explain the product. Typically, you don't need to go into too much detail when it comes to the product. The main idea is not to sell the product itself but to sell the investment and the potential that comes with it. You also always sell yourself as the expert and therefore the product becomes less important. Because if you have properly positioned yourself as the expert, then your advice should not be questioned.

Technique 1: Give me your initial trust

I understand that you cannot give me 100% of your trust at this point in time. That is why I only want 5% of your trust. The remaining 95% I will have to work for. Please give me a chance to prove to you how great I am at my job and I can promise you that you will not be disappointed. But there is one thing I expect. If we have done this deal successfully, I want you to refer me to other people and open up a bottle of wine with me to celebrate all the money that I made for you, agreed?

Technique 2: Setting the amount high initially

- Would it be possible for you to free up $100,000 over the next few weeks?
- No, what dollar amount would be possible for you?
- Is $50,000 possible?
- No, why don't we make a small trial deal to get to know each other? You can test me and my firm and our ability to make you money?
- Let me give you the story again . . .

Technique 3: Golden spoon

- These kinds of opportunities don't come along every day. The current situation in market is so special that we need to take advantage of it now. You won't regret it.
- Mr. client, I can only hand you the sugar with the golden spoon but you will have to take it. Shall we invest $10,000 or $20,000?

- Mr. client, just give it a try. You did realize that you could make lots of money with this deal, right? The money is in the streets and I can tell you exactly where it is right now. All you have to do is to pick it up. Are you going to invest $10,000 or $20,000 now?

Technique 4: Your stock recommendation from last week

Use small talk and stories to find out the real reason why he is hesitant.

- We had spoken last week and I had given you a stock tip. Did you see how much the stock rose in the meantime? (A different stock)
- Now I am about to tell you about a similar tip (the stock that you want to sell).

Explaining the market:

- Based on all the facts that I just outlined and explained to you, I am sure you can see the potential and value of this company.

If no, what did you not yet understand? Where did I not make it clear?

Closing:

- In such market conditions professional investors always invest at least 100,000 shares, amateurs take 30,000 and beginners try it with 10,000 shares. Where do you see yourself? (Don't talk further, let him answer)
- After he has given you his number, go straight into the contract as if it was a done deal and without asking whether he wants it or not.

- Well in that case I am going to reserve X amount of shares for you. To which email address shall I send you the contract?

If he still refuses or is unsure:

- With this kind of business it is not the question whether you should invest or not. The question is only how much you should invest. How much money do you want to make?
- Take his number and triple it. That is the investment sum that he should invest.

Technique 5: His response: "I need to think about it, I can't make a decision now."

- Mr. Client, my job is of course to look at each deal as objectively as possible and to be able to answer all your questions as thoroughly as possible. I am sure you still have questions or concerns that are not yet 100% clear to you. Now you have the opportunity to talk to me and I am an absolute professional in this field. Which factors are still not quite clear?

The only thing holding him back is lack of trust and fear. Move the focus away from the contract for a while and talk about other subjects. It is important to focus more on the relationship and on building trust. Use stories; change the mood by laughing or telling a funny joke. Use metaphors to explain why it makes sense to act today.

Technique 6: Doing the contract

- The procedure must be very clear and must be explained in detail to the client so that there is no confusion or misunderstanding.

- Mr. Client, in order to do this deal you will only need three things: a working pen, five minutes of your time and your email account (or fax).
- Do you have this? Yes? Very good.
- I will send you the share subscription agreement now and I am asking you to sign it and immediately send it back, please. Is that ok? What is your email address or fax number please?
- Call him back in 5 minutes.

Technique 7: A businessman makes decisions

- Mr. Client, as a business man you are used to making quick and important decisions, right? Because if you were a regular employee and average person you would not be able to be in life where you are today.
- And to make the decision to invest $20,000 today isn't really the biggest decision that you had to make in your business and personal life, correct?
- So in that case, this is a small decision for you that you can make right away.

Objection 1: I have no money

- Mr. Client, based on your business profile you have 20 employees in your company and you need to pay them a salary every month. So if your average monthly salary is $5000, then your employee cost alone is over $100,000 per month. If you include other costs, this number might be double. And you want to tell me that you have no money? Come on . . . you don't need to tell me stories. I know you have the ability to free up money if you really want. $10,000 or $20,000 is small change for you. Let me show you what really is in it for you if you invest into this deal.
- What do you mean by "no money"? For one person $100,000 is no money for another person it is a lot. How much money can you free up in the next 1 to 2 months if

you sell some of your other positions where you are only losing money?

Objection 2: I have no interest

- How much do you know about this industry and products in detail? Do you have profound knowledge about it? No? In that case it is very normal not to have any interest because you simply don't understand yet what the real potential for you could be. Let me explain a bit more . . .
- I can understand that. Most of our clients had no interest at first when we talked about it. But once I was able to help them understand how much money they could make with it, they were happy that they continued to listen.

Objection 3: I have no time

- My time is also limited. Therefore, I suggest we make an appointment for 30 minutes where I can really explain to you how you can make money. Which day of this week would work best for you?
- Most people work too much and forget to make money because of all the time that they waste on their job. Please let us not make the same mistake. By utilizing your time efficiently and in a smart way, you can make much more money than just simply going to work. Let me show you how . . .

Objection 4: Too risky

- You will risk a few dollars but I will risk my whole career. Do you believe that I will gamble with my career? Of course not.
- It is only risk if you don't know what you are doing. This is why you have me as your advisor. I know exactly what we are doing and how to make you money. I don't do risky

things. I analyze the investment and take all the risk out of it.

- The people who risked something in life are in our history books. The ones who never risked anything are all forgotten.

With new or first time clients we always pick a stock where we know for sure that the risk is limited. We want to make you happy with our first deal so that you will become a long-term client.

Objection 5: I am in the process of building a house

- Would you have to stop building your house if it cost you $20,000 more? No? Well there is no problem.
- Great decision, congratulations. But a successful businessman like you would not build a house with the last dollar that he has available, right? So how much security do you still have available?
- How much is the mortgage on your house? $500,000. Do you want to find out how you can get rid of that debt in half of the time?

Objection 6: My tax consultant says no

- I didn't expect any other answer. Your tax consultant is a specialist when it comes to tax questions. In this case we are talking about investments and not taxes. And your tax consultant is not a broker or investment professional. If he advised you to invest into any investment, he could only lose credibility and his license. So therefore he will never advise you to invest in anything at all.
- Do you ask your electrician for advise when you buy a car? No? Well that is the same thing here. Your tax advisor is not a stockbroker.

Objection 7: My banker says no

- Any banker has to recommend the products that the bank offers or otherwise he will lose his job. He will never recommend a product that comes from the competition.
- Most bankers have no idea about Private Equity products because they don't have the education in this field. Therefore, they automatically will disregard what they don't understand. Because if he really understood this business, he would be investing into it himself instead of trying to sell you another bank product like a credit card or a money market account.
- Why do you listen to the advice of a regular person who is employed by a bank and probably only makes $60,000 per year? This person is not financially successful and does not know how to really make money. So why listen to a loser rather than someone who is financially successful himself?

Objection 8: My wife says no

- Are you in charge of your business or is it your wife? You? Well, then you can make that decision alone. Just like you make all other business decisions alone.

Objection 9: Don't feel like doing it

- These are the exact words of my three year old son when I ask him to eat his spinach! He doesn't feel like it but we both know that it is very good for him.
- Your feeling has nothing to do with this investment. This is a business decision and nothing else.

Objection 10: I have lost money before

- It is like a child who burned his fingers. You burned your fingers once but now you know how not to burn your fingers again.

- Did you ever buy fruit from the grocery store before and when you got home you realized that it was already bad? And because of this you stopped eating fruit altogether? No? Well, then it was unfortunate but it doesn't mean that all investments are like the one where you lost money. This is a completely different type of fruit (investment) anyway.

General statements that help to convince investors

- If this train leaves, it is hard to get back on later. And there is not another one coming that is going where you want to go.
- When it comes to stocks, it is important when you get in and when you get out. Now is exactly the right time to get in. I will let you know when to get out, too.
- If you sleep on it, you won't be smarter tomorrow. If you knew what I know about this deal, you wouldn't hesitate one second.
- How much time do you need to think about it? 2 weeks? So are you going to think about it for 2 hours for the next 14 days? So a total of 28 hours? I don't think so. That would be ridiculous, right? So how much real thinking time do you really need? One hour? So let me help you right now. If you still need time, then I will call you tomorrow morning.
- All wealthy people without exception own a stock portfolio.
- Do you have a sign at your door that says: "Closed because of too much wealth"?
- I am sorry if I am putting too much pressure on you right now. But you need to understand that you can buy a car and wait a couple of weeks before you actually get it. But when it comes to stocks, one day or even one hour can make a difference whether you make 100% return or only 1%. That is why I urge you to act now.
- Trust is the basis for every relationship. Don't you agree? And when it comes to investing I am sure that you want a partner that you can trust 100%, right? Assuming you

knew me very well you trusted me completely, would there be anything else that you would have to know right now in regards to the investment?

- The only certain thing in life is death and taxes. Otherwise there are no guarantees. I cannot predict the future. I can only tell you from my 20 years of experience in the stock market that I have analyzed this company from top to bottom and I have never seen such a great deal in my whole career.

- If you can buy a BMW today for $40,000 and you know that the exact same car will cost you $60,000 tomorrow then you wouldn't wait, would you?

- Diversification is a protection against the unknown. Diversification doesn't make sense for people who know what they are doing. That is why I only invest into companies that are fundamentally undervalued.

- If a stock is popular, everybody is looking at it. But the time to pick a stock is before it is popular. Do you know the company XYZ Oil? No? Well check out the chart. It went up 500% in the last 12 months. Nobody knows this company. You didn't know about it, either. And here I present you with ABC Oil. Another deal that will go through the roof but yet again no one has heard about it yet.

- The dice have been rolled in New York. This deal will be a winner.

- Right now we have an advantage to the masses. We have information that is not publicly known yet. We need to use this information now before everybody else has it, too.

- Information is the main key when it comes to making investment decisions.

- I will do my best for you. Not just 100% but 200%.

- I have never played Russian roulette in the stock market. I will not invest into anything that is based on pure luck or chance.

- Investing is just like jumping into an ice cold pool. You go in with confidence but you don't stay for too long.

- People who own interest-bearing investments sleep well but people who own stocks live well.

- You will get rich if you invest into companies that cost less than they are valued at.
- Let's look at your situation right now. It can't get any worse than it currently is. It can only get better. And here is how . . .
- If you buy a stock when you believe that all the risks have been avoided you are buying it too late.
- When you are young you believe that money is everything. Only when you get old you realize that it really was everything.
- When things are bad in the stock market most people will refrain from investing. But this is exactly the time when the biggest riches are created. You need to be smart and not follow the masses.
- There are only two options to make money: You either work for it or your money works for you.
- Sometimes it is smarter to think about investing for a few hours instead of working for it a whole month.
- People who constantly hesitate will never achieve anything.

Understanding the psychology behind objections

Objection example: I have no interest

Real meaning:

You have failed to make the client curious. Curiosity is key when first dealing with new investors. You will have to make a statement that will tackle his curiosity. The second reason might be that he is scared. In this case you will have to take out any kind of risk. The first approach with any new client has to be a non-threatening first contact. People are afraid that you will sell them something and that they are forced into something that they don't want.

You could say something like:

"I totally understand that you have no interest at this point in time. That is normal. I would suggest that it would be best if I will send you some general information that you can look at and then you can decide if you think this could be interesting for you. Does that sound fair?"

The question at the end "Does that sound fair?" is a trick question. The question in itself will force the client to say yes. The proposal is of course fair. There is no other answer possible.

The main goal in the beginning is to simply get a first contact established. Once you have sent him some information you have a reason to call him back. Sending him information is non-threatening and there is no obligation for him to do anything.

You can also say this:

"Mr. Smith, almost all of my clients have reacted exactly the same way like you just did. They also had no interest at first. But once they looked at the material and talked to me for a short period of time, they all realized how much money they could make. So let me make a suggestion: Why don't I send you some general information about a deal for you to study. And if you want to talk further, then we can talk. If not, no harm done. Does that sound fair?"

Another option is:

"I can understand your reaction because you simply don't know yet what this is all about. Therefore I would suggest the following: I will send you some information for you to look at and you can still decide later whether this is of interest to you or not. Does that sound fair?"

Stay positive

Objections are a normal part of the selling process. Don't get discouraged and welcome objections positively and with open arms. Say things like: Oh, Mr. Client, I knew you were going to say that! Ha, ha!

> Most people don't want to buy anything at first!

Try two or three rebuttals with clients but if you feel that you are not getting anywhere, let them go and focus on the next client. You need to protect your integrity and your own motivation. If there is one person who is overly negative he might destroy your motivation and spirit and you won't be able to talk to other clients with the same enthusiasm. You don't need negative people in your life. Sometimes it is better not to do a deal with someone if you get the feeling that this person will be difficult or trouble in the future. Interestingly, it is always the person who invested $5000 who can make your life hell. It is never the one who invested $100,000.

How do you deal with objections?

> An objection is nothing but a question. It
> shows that the person is interested.
> The rule is: no objections = no interest

Try to identify the real reason behind objections. If someone says that they have no money, it might not necessarily be true. They might be afraid to lose money or they feel that the little money that they have is not enough for an investment.

Always try to prepare and answer potential objections in advance. It is ok to mention negative features of a product if you say them first. By doing this you will take away the persons argument later and he can't bring it up again.

Make a list of all the potential objections that clients bring up and prepare written answers. Learn those answers by heart so that you are better prepared when they come. The objections are always more or less the same and they are:

- I have no interest
- I have no money
- I have no time
- I already have a financial advisor
- I have lost money before
- This is too risky for me
- I already have a tax consultant
- I don't buy stocks over the phone
- I need to ask my wife
- I don't like this industry, product or the terms
- I need to think about it / sleep on it

Try to put yourself into the shoes of the client. Develop a feeling for the client's situation. Try to identify how the client feels and what concerns he might have. Develop your level of emotional intelligence. By working on this you will become a much better sales person.

Identify yourself with the product that you are selling. Sales people who believe in the product usually get far fewer objections than people who have doubts themselves. No one wants to make a deal with a person who has doubts himself.

You can also use all the rhetorical techniques in the world and "win" every argument with the client but if you lose the person, you won't be able to make a sale. Great sales people use techniques as well but only in such a manner that you cannot easily identify them as sales techniques. Great sales people use a lot of statements that trigger emotions.

Never try to convince a client or talk them into investing. Pressuring someone will backfire almost every time. Try to create a situation where the client wants to buy. Now how do you do that? It can take some time to prepare a situation. First, you need to develop a trust relationship with a client. Don't talk about the product right away. Make him curious and position yourself as the absolute expert. Most great sales people talk about everything else but the product in the first two hours. Once they have figured out the client and know how to influence him, they will bring up the product later. Some sales people talk 95% about life and everything else and then spend 5% on the product. They don't get any objections because it is a logical consequence that the client will invest and there is no question whether the sales person has picked the right product or not. A lot of great sales people don't even need the marketing material or website. It is all based on the trust relationship.

A lot of great sales people try to find a deficit in the client's situation and then build this up and develop almost a problem situation for the client. Once the client is afraid, they will present the product as the solution to fix that problem and the client is happy.

The second call with the client

After you have established the initial contact with the client and you have sent him some general information about your company, you can call him up again and that is where the real sales process starts.

Here is a short version of a potential second call:

- Hello, my name is John Smith. I am calling from ABC Financial.
- You have spoken with my assistant Mrs. Nice and she has sent you some material about the company XYZ. Did you have a chance to study the material?
- No? That is ok. I will be happy to give you some more information about it later. But first I would like to introduce myself properly.
- My name is John Smith and I have been a financial professional for the last 20 years. I have an MBA from the University of New York and today I am a specialist in high finance investments.
- Mr. Client, do you know what high finance is exactly?
- No? That's ok. Let me explain. You take your money to the bank and what does your bank actually do with the money?
- They invest it into other things like loans, mortgages and special investments.
- That's right. They use your money and invest it for themselves. How much return do you think they can make? 10—20%? Correct.
- And how much do they give you back? 1 to 2%.
- So the bank invests into projects with your money and doesn't let you participate.
- You see, we do things differently. We have access to great investments just like the bank and we let you participate in the returns directly and fully.
- This is high finance.
- Now normally, my clients have a portfolio of at least $1 million with me and I wonder how you were able to actually land on my table so that I gave you a call.
- Maybe this is your lucky day . . .

The main thing at this point is to position yourself as an absolute expert and that you have the ability to create great returns for your clients.

- Now let me tell you a little bit about our company.
- ABC Financial is the global leader when it comes to Private Equity investments in the resource sector. We have many satisfied clients that we have worked with over many years. All of our clients are very wealthy and we only have long-term relationships.
- Our research department in New York analyzes hundreds of companies every month and picks out only the best deals with the greatest potentials. We have been able to give our clients returns that are way above the average because we pick and choose from the best of the best.
- We have sent you some information about the oil industry. Do you know why oil is such a great investment right now?
- Here are the reasons . . .

Again. You position yourself and your company in such a way that the feels that it is his lucky day. You don't really have to talk about the product at all at this point in time. Don't try to sell him anything yet. Focus on positioning and on the relationship. Continue the conversation with asking questions about the client. Ask as much as you can and develop a positive and friendly atmosphere.

After a while you can continue with talking about the advantages of Private Equity and why it makes sense to invest into a pre-IPO deal. Give him all the positive reasons.

Here is a short list:

- It will never be as cheap as it is now.
- He will be able to double or triple his investment at the IPO.
- The potential of the stock price can be even higher and at several dollars per share.
- Talk about the industry and why it makes sense.
- Give him examples of other deals that have gone through the roof.

- Mention a specific project or area that is very promising without giving away the deal name.
- Tell him that you might be able to find a similar project with all those features.
- Tell him how smaller companies always outperform larger companies.
- Talk about the volume and promotion once the company is listed and that you have the ability to help him to get out at the right point in time.
- Give him example of Microsoft, Yahoo or Google who nobody knew at first and that they are now huge companies. Tell him that you believe that this new deal could potentially be similar.

The main thing is to explain the process and the features of Private Equity. You can wait with giving him the actual product and make him curious. Remember:

> The most curious animal in the world
> is not the cat. It is the human.

Build him up so that he can't wait for your call in a few days. Tell him that you will be looking for a project like you just described and that you will get back to him in a few days.

Third call

The third call will be much easier than the second. You have already established a trust relationship and he will be curious to hear what you have to say.

Now, it is important to use the following techniques:

- Make the product rare / unavailable for the average person

- Limit the amount of shares available for him
- Tell him the price of the financing round will go up next week
- Put on a time pressure to act (maximum 24 to 48 hours)
- Use high numbers starting at $100,000 +

If everybody can have the product, it will lose its attractiveness and the client will lose interest. If it is available in a month for the same price, then there is no reason for him to act now. You need to make it rare and you need to use urgency otherwise you will never close the deal. Without those two techniques you are doomed to fail. I have seen it many times.

Now always start at a high number like $100,000. Don't be afraid to use that number. You can even have a minimum investment sum like $100,000 mentioned in your PPM (Private Placement Memorandum). And then you can make an exception by letting him invest only $50,000.

The main goal at this point is to close the deal. Get him to sign the contract and transfer the money as soon as possible. The whole sales process from the initial contact to the actual transfer of the money usually takes 3 to 4 weeks anyway.

Becoming a Private Equity Broker

Starting your career as a Private Equity broker

A Private Equity broker finances start-up companies that are private and then takes them public. A typical financing amount ranges from $2 to $20 million per company.

The main objective is to raise money for companies by selling shares of private companies to investors and to take the company public. The goal is to make money for your investors by getting them into a low entry point and getting them out at a high profit.

When a company is listed on a stock exchange, it is considered to be a public company. When it is not yet listed, it is called a private company. The term "Equity" simply refers to stocks.

In the long run, stocks usually outperform any other asset classes and smaller companies can develop much more in value in the beginning. A big company like McDonald's is unlikely to double in price within one year but a small start-up company can double, triple or grow even further.

When looking at a stock chart, it is only possible to see the first price when the company was first listed. The company however has been around for a longer period of time and usually got financed through private financings. These financing rounds are called private placements. If a company does a first round of financing at for example $0.40 a share, it might raise capital for future business development. The company might continue to raise capital by using several financing rounds before it goes public. These rounds may be at the $0.50, $0.65 or the $0.80 level. The general public will only then be able to buy stocks when the company is listed at $1.00 for example. But investors who were able to buy the stocks for $0.40 per share have already more than doubled their money.

The advantages of Private Equity are that there are no price fluctuations, are able to participate in the beginning of a new venture when the price of a share is at its cheapest, have a high return on investment potential and a relatively short investment horizon of only 6 to 24 months.

Private Equity brokers are selling shares to accredited (wealthy) private investors of companies that are not yet listed or trading. The transaction is called Private Placement and is an offer to purchase shares of private companies. The plan is to finance companies that will eventually go public in a stock market (IPO = Initial public offering). You can offer your investors several attractive investment possibilities a year with a chance of getting high returns.

However, not every Private Equity deal is a success. It is possible that some deals fail but others go through the roof. That is why it is wise to invest into a series of different projects to spread the risk and get a diversification of the portfolio.

Private Equity is considered a high-risk type of investment. This is the case because new companies have a higher risk to go bankrupt. In fact 85% of new companies fail in the first three years. The main reasons are 1. Lack of capital, 2. Poor management and 3. Bad products with no market.

The best way to ensure success is to focus on the financing and building the share structure for companies that will enable you to take it public, put in experienced management and only chose products that you believe to be a great success in the market.

For example, if you simply gave $5 million to a scientist who invented a great product, it is not ensured that the company will be successful. The scientist may be great in his area of expertise but he may simply lack management skills, financial knowledge, marketing skills, etc. and may not know how to make a company successful in the stock market.

Therefore, you need to keep a close control over the company in the beginning to ensure that it goes into the right direction.

By doing so, you protect the interests of our investors until they have an exit.

You should invest in a variety of industries. I would mainly focus on resources, biotechnology, life science, real estate or technology projects. The decision to finance a particular project is dependent on several factors and I would not be open to most industries.

When you are putting together a new project, a series of factors need to be considered: the shell (corporation), management team, financing, specialist team (e.g. geological team), projects or products, legal counsel, administrational support, accounting, financial knowledge, investor relations, contact of networks, strategic action plan and exit for investors.

When you are considering a new project, you need to determine whether the project will be a success in the future. We have to decide if the company's products or services will actually be marketable, what the quality standards are, if distribution channels need to be established, what the financing requirements will be and if the stock will have sufficient trading volume in the market. Only if all these factors can be answered positively, you should agree to finance a new project.

Job description

The main objective of the job is to get investors to buy shares of private companies—basically to raise money. The job is sales and relationship focused because the broker is dealing with clients. The broker will sell shares to clients and advise them on how to invest into Private Equity. There is lots of telephone activity involved because clients live all over the country.

A broker will establish a lot of client contacts and will have lots of face-to-face meetings with investors. He will make investment recommendations and grow a client base over time.

Typically, a broker will do about 100 telephone calls per day and will be able to send out about ten information packages to potential clients. Out of these ten potential clients, he may get one prospect in the end.

The goal is to build up a number of clients that will invest into several deals. A client will invest into one deal at first, grow his investment and then invest into more deals in the future. By having successful deals, the broker will not only grow his client base but also the money under management.

In order to advise clients on investments, a Private Equity Broker will need to be licensed with FINRA and pass the Series 7 and 63 exams in the US.

The problem with FINRA is that you are very closely supervised and that it is almost impossible to promote a company positively because of all the laws that have been created. Being a licensed broker can be a pain and actually work to your disadvantage. Another problem is that you will have to get sponsored by a broker dealer who is a member of FINRA. Otherwise you cannot take the exams.

There is also another solution. If you build your own company and you are a director of the company you are legally allowed to raise capital. As part of the management team you can say how great you think the company is and you are a direct representative of the company. This is a loophole and is much better than being licensed.

A broker will build a client portfolio of private investors and will eventually trade stocks in the market on behalf of the client. He will earn a commission on capital raised and by selling shares. If the broker raises for example $100,000 per month from private investors, he can earn anywhere from 5% to 10% in commission based on his career level. Additionally, brokers also get shares in the deals that they finance which can be very lucrative if a deal goes really well.

A new broker should have a solid education with a university degree in finance, business administration, economics or similar. But the most important thing to succeed in this industry, however, is the personality of a broker. A candidate should be outgoing, communicative, extroverted, smart, ethical, driven and open to learn something new. He should have an interest in the financial industry and to build long-term client relationships.

Since it is not an easy challenge in the beginning, a candidate should be aware that he might face a number of difficult situations. A broker has to deal with a lot of rejection and needs to be determined to succeed. Especially in the beginning of his career until someone has built up a substantial client base, there is a lot of prospecting involved.

Advantages of being a Private Equity Broker

A Private Equity Broker offers a number of interesting investments that only he can offer. No other firm will be able to offer the specific products that he can offer.

The specific knowledge that a Private Equity Broker obtains is worth millions of dollars. This knowledge will enable someone to create new companies and to create value in the stock market beyond a normal scope.

The difference to a regular stockbroker, who gathers assets, is speed and earning potential. Just like a "normal" stockbroker, who is trying to get investors to invest their money with him, a Private Equity Broker needs to raise capital. A regular broker will invest the money into stocks, bonds and mutual funds and get a sales commission for it. Typically, this commission is around 2% of the amount invested. The broker will then have to share the commission with the brokerage firm and will end up with about 1% of the money invested. In the long run, a regular stockbroker who is doing portfolio management will also be able to make a lot of money but it usually takes about three years to be in a comfortable situation. The earning process is very slow and the beginning is hard.

A Private Equity Broker on the other hand, will earn anywhere from 5% to 10% on money raised and will earn a lot more money right from the start. Companies pay a higher commission of about 10% for Private Equity financings because they are in need of money and without it they cannot further develop their business.

Once someone starts, it is expected that someone actively generate leads in the first month. The trainee should make at least 100 new client introductions. The goal is to build up a number of referrals from existing contacts to create a pool of potential investors. Doing cold calling however is not an easy task in America these days. People have caller ID or they are fed up with too many solicitors trying to sell them something. Therefore it is important to have a good contact list and work strictly with referrals. Once a client is happy with your service he will refer you to other potential clients and that is the best way to be successful in this business.

Being a Private Equity Broker

Becoming a Private Equity Broker is an exciting adventure. Like-minded people who also want to succeed in life surround you. If you have a great team of individuals that are go-getters and great communicators, you will be excited to go to work every day.

You are able to offer new and interesting investment opportunities to your clients on a regular basis and you will build long-term relationships. You will not only make money for your investors but also make money for yourself.

Initially, when deals are still private, you will mainly focus on meeting clients and advising them how to invest. After deals are trading on a stock market however, you will also start trading shares in the market.

You can help with the creation of new projects and really learn the business of private equity financing. This will give you the possibility to make a lot of money in the future.

Once you have established successful client relationships you will move them from one deal into the next and keep them happy. Therefore you will grow not only your client base but also your investments under management. Eventually, you will be managing millions of dollars for your clients and you will be able to finance deals on your own.

The sky is the limit and there are a lot of opportunities in this business and in the world. There will always be people who will make investments no matter how bad the economy seems to be.

Ideal plan for a Private Equity broker

- Setting new meetings per day: 4
- Actually doing 3 meetings per day because one gets cancelled, moved or is the wrong person
- Total meetings per week: 15
- Read one book about sales and marketing
- Read one book about investments and finance
- Read one book about personal development
- Finding the right names, lists, people to contact
- Getting referrals from personal network
- Practicing the presentation
- Improving telephone skills and objections
- Putting together a binder with information for investors
- Mandatory reading material: How to win friends and influence people by Dale Carnegie
- A hugely important factor in sales is motivation. What motivates you the most? What do you want to buy for yourself? How much money do you need to make?
- Focus your time on product knowledge so that you become an absolute specialist in this field.

Ideal target per month

1. $200,000 in money raised—10 to 15% in commission = $20,000 to $30,000 in salary
2. 30 FMs (First Meetings)
3. 20 SMs (Second Meetings = selling)
4. 100 IPs (Information packages) sent out by cold calling

Becoming the best

You need to understand that this is one of the most difficult jobs that are out there. Selling investments over the phone to people that don't know you can be quite the challenge. Unfortunately, not everybody is cut out for it. 80% of the people who start in this industry fail in the first three months because they are not closing any deals. If you are willing to learn and grow and never give up, you can potentially turn into a great sales person. People in this industry who have decided to become the best can easily make more than one million dollars per year.

Most people are holding themselves back because of fear of rejection, fear of failure and laziness.

This industry is really tricky. Once you get hooked, you will never get out of the industry. You might change companies but it is very hard to change the profession once you were successful once. People who made the experience of earning $20,000 or $50,000 in a month will never go back to a regular job that pays $5,000 or $10,000 a month. Once you have figured out how it works you will never have to worry about money again. If you know how to sell Private Equity and you have a good product to sell, you can always make a lot of money in a short period of time and turn your life around. It is almost like a secret knowledge that you must obtain and you must have experienced a phase where you made a lot of money. Once this is the case you can always go back to selling private stocks—no matter where you are in life.

Business Development

Business models for Private Equity

There are a number of industries and products that go well with Private Equity. In general, you should choose a business model that has a huge potential for growth. What do I mean by that? If you are in the restaurant business and you believe that you could go public with your restaurant that has $1 million in sales, then you should not consider it at all. You should only choose business models that can create a valuation of $500 million to $1 billion over the next five years.

Everything that is valued under $100 million in the stock market is considered a micro-cap company.

Good choices are:

1. Precious metals and natural resources (like gold, silver, copper, etc.)
2. Oil and gas
3. Biotechnology
4. Technology and communication
5. Real Estate

Difficult industries if start-ups:

In general, there is no bad industry or no business model that could not be public. There are however industries or products that will have a more difficult start than others. Software, for example, is a difficult topic because there might be a better software or version available from China 6 months down the road, which would make the product obsolete. A new kind of telephone or technology device would be hard to sell because you would first have to develop the actual market and need for the product, which would take about 5 years and cost millions of dollars in marketing expenses just to make the product known.

Example: Gold

A better or easier solution is precious metals. Let's take gold for example. You can acquire an option for a piece of land for $20,000 and then spend $1 million in exploration cost trying to find gold and to do drilling. If you have found 500,000 ounces of gold and the gold price is at $1500, then you overall potential and value is $750 million for your company. By having luck or finding the right project, you can create value out of nothing because you will get the gold from mother earth for free.

If you had to produce an actual product you would have costs for production, storage, transportation, marketing, etc. Natural resources are so much easier because everybody needs them and they are already traded on different market places all over the world.

Example: Oil

Oil and gas is great because the more projects that you have, the more monthly cash flow you create. Example: If you invest about $1 million into a project that has proven oil reserves and you can produce 100 barrels per day at $100 per barrel, then your monthly gross cash flow is $300,000, which would lead to about $150,000 net cash flow.

If you have 5 projects producing 100 bbl (barrels) each your annual earnings would be $1.8 million x 5 = $9 million.

If your P/E ratio is 10, then your market capitalization is $90 million.

The great thing about oil and gas is that now the company can use the annual proceeds and invest them into other new wells and projects that will produce oil, too. Because most projects only need an initial investment and then can produce for the next 10 to 20 years, it is almost impossible for the company to go out of business as long as there is a global need for oil.

Example: Biotechnology

Biotechnology is also a great business model but expensive to finance. Typically, a company has an idea for a new medication that needs to go through the FDA process. The FDA has 3 phases.

Phase 1: A product or a substance is being tested with 10-20 people and the main focus is on potential risks and side effects. Initial cost: $500,000 to $1 million.

Phase 2: The product will be given to more clients and the cost will be about $5 to $10 million.

Phase 3: The product will go into its final stage and it will take about $20 to $30 million to finance this phase.

Once phase 3 is finished and the product is approved by the FDA, it will be worth anywhere from $500 million to $1 billion depending on what it is and the company is a takeover target for a big pharmaceutical company.

If you are interested in biotech, then you should go to a University and try to find some PhD students or professors who are working on developing a new cure or medication. Their problem is that they have a theory but no access to funding. That is where you can come in.

You might not know anything about biotechnology or medicine but you could take those professors and make them your management team. Your job is to finance the company and take it public. Typically, you only need to get to phase 2 to become a potential takeover candidate for a bigger company.

Business development and going public

When you are developing a new deal, you have basically two main things to worry about:

1. Business development
2. Going public process and financing

First you need to have a business or a business idea to get started. You need to have a business model with a business plan that you want to develop. Based on that you can figure out how much capital you will require to make it a reality.

So the business always comes first. The goal is to create a business that has a lot of value and that has potential to continue to grow. Based on that valuation and potential you can calculate what the value in the stock market will be.

You can either develop a product or service that has a unit price and that is sold to many customers. This will generate sales and earnings. The goal is then to develop the company further and expand its operations so that you will increase the sales and earnings each year.

The second method is to acquire a project that seems to have a lot of potential and speculate that it will have a lot of resources on it (like it is the case for gold or oil). Based on your drilling results you will discover a resource that will all of a sudden add several hundred millions of dollars to your company.

A third way is to develop a new medication or cure. This cure once proven successful and being approved by the FDA will then add value in the hundreds of millions to your deal.

Basically, it will take a few years to develop a solid business model and to create a real value in a company. But that doesn't mean that you can't start from scratch and with no money and only an idea or vision.

A lot of people made a lot of money with only an idea or vision and because there was only future potential and no real value in the company yet, the stock went up. If people believe in a concept and if the market is willing to pay for it, then the value will be high and stock price will go up.

You can also just simply do a lot of stock marketing and promotion for your company and create a lot of buyers in your stock. Your stock will then attract more and more attention from the market and will continue to go up even though there might not be any kind of value in the company yet. It will solely be based on speculation and future potential. But that is ok as long as the company is working on making the business a reality.

While you are developing your business model and products you will need to go through the SEC process to get public. You will have to file your S-1 registration statement with the SEC, do your private placements, raise money by finding investors, file your form 15c2-11 with the market maker to get your trading symbol so that you are ready to be public and then eventually attract institutional financing.

Sometimes it is easier to get the process going of developing your public shell and then to merge a good business model into it.

It is important to understand the difference between the people and the skills that are required to make this whole company a success. You will need technical people who will operate and develop the project and then you will finance people who will raise money and take the company public.

Fraud and ethics

Once you understand the process of taking a company public and then selling shares into the market, you will realize that this knowledge or skill alone will be enough to become a millionaire. You can finance a deal, get commission, take it public and then sell your share position into the open market and make a lot of money. In this case you don't care what the business does or what its development is.

There are a lot of people who operate like that. They care very little about the actual operation and they only care about themselves. Often, they get carried away and create a pump and dump scenario where the business or the assets in the company are basically non-existent or worthless. But they promote it like they were very valuable.

Unfortunately, there is no real rule of ethics or moral when it comes to public companies. You can always argue that your deal or project has a lot of potential and it is very hard to prove otherwise.

There are a lot of people who follow the SEC and FINRA rules and are 100% legal. But in reality they are taking advantage of naïve investors and they sell them something that has no real value.

It is up to you to decide how you want to operate and develop your company. If you choose the quick way then at least be 100% legal and compliant with the law. Become a specialist or hire good lawyers who will make sure that you follow all rules. And there are a lot of rules today.

It is possible to make a lot of money pre-IPO as well as post IPO even if the company itself isn't successful. But the main problem with this strategy is that it will only work once or twice. You will lose your reputation and trust in your investors and it will take a lot of new investors to do a new deal. In general, you are only as good as your last deal.

Once you had a bad deal, and almost everybody does, it is very hard to recover from it financially and emotionally. Today, with the Internet, people will destroy your name and make sure that you will have a hard time finding new investors for a new deal even if it was not your fault that the stock went down. Sometimes a bad promoter or partner or short seller put so much pressure on your stock price that you had no chance and the share price fell down into a downward spiral of sellers.

Therefore I urge you to focus on a real business model that generates money and that can be successful even if the stock price is falling. If you own a real piece in a good deal, then your share position is real and valuable and not just based on a theoretical valuation.

The plan should be to combine a good plan with an aggressive money raising strategy. Make sure that you will keep some shares in the company and don't sell off all of your position. Develop the business to a certain phase so that it is eligible for institutional financing and that the company will get $20 to $50 million to expand and grow even further. If that is the case, then you will have real value in the company and it will only be a matter of time until your shares are more valuable.

After the initial set-up of the company

After you have set-up the company, acquired a project, hired a management team and raised the first funds, it is time to start to develop a plan for the company.

The company will need to do the following things:

1. Going public—ensure enough financing to pay for auditors, legal fees, etc. (approximately $200,000)
2. Acquisition of more projects or bigger projects to justify a higher future valuation in the stock market
3. Expanding the management team and advisory board to increase the overall profile of experts
4. Expansion—Increasing sales, revenue and valuation
5. Developing a marketing plan for the public company to promote the shares and creating new buying volume in the market
6. Financing—ensure proper pre-IPO financing through private investors and post-IPO financing through institutional investors
7. Developing the company from a start-up company to a more established company
8. Listing on a larger stock exchange and co-Listing on a foreign stock market
9. Selling a certain amount of shares for the management team into the market and turning it into cash
10. Creating an exit scenario for initial investors

Time frame

It is typical that it will take about 6 to 9 months for the SEC and FINRA to approve your S-1 Filing and to get your company trading. Therefore, I would suggest that you have a plan for the first 12 months that looks as follows:

- Acquire flag ship project / product for the company
- Develop a proof of concept
- Get audited financial statements
- File S-1 registration statement with the SEC
- File form 15c2-11 with FINRA (done by market maker)
- Raise enough capital for administration, legal fees, audit fees, management fees, initial project costs, marketing budget and enough money for the first few months after the listing to be able to continue operations.

Budget / financing needs

It really depends on the kind of business that you are operating how much money you should raise in the first year while your company is still private. Typically, the initial budget is from $500,000 to about $2 million. The more money you have, the quicker you can develop your company and its projects and the faster you will be able to get a higher valuation. So raising money is absolute key. Most businesses fail because of lack of money in the first few years.

Your goal should be to develop your products to such a degree that you won't be dependent on outside capital to continue your operations. Once you have hit this milestone you have "proof of concept". This is very important because you will then also have "proof of management", which means that your team was able to get the company from phase A to phase B. If your industry and business model is in demand, it should be very easy at this point to secure additional financing for your company. The hardest part is always to get the first $2 million dollars. That is why you need to primarily raise them through private investors in the beginning. Once you have done that and taken the company public you will be able to get a financing of $5 to $25 million easily based on your company's products. All you have to do is to duplicate your efforts and expand the company's business model.

Marketing plan, business development and exit strategy

The main goal of this plan is to achieve a market capitalization of at least $100 million over the next 24 months.

Another major goal is to have a successful exit for all initial investors, so that they are willing to continue to work with you and to use their capital for the next project.

Typical company goals for a start-up deal

1. Public listing in 12 months
2. $0.50 opening price
3. Development of price strategy to $1.00 per share and later $2.00
4. Market capitalization of $50 million at listing
5. Seed and first round investors to get an exit strategy
6. Strategy for management to make money without hurting shareholders and price
7. Creation of enough volume for 25 million shares to be sold within 24 months
8. Fulfill requirements of NYSE AMEX listing
9. Development of marketing strategy
10. Business Development and milestones for the company

Going public process—overview

1. Financial Statements (FS) need to be created by corporate accountant
2. FS need to be audited

3. Securities lawyer prepares and file S-1 Registration Statement with the SEC
4. Comments from the SEC need to be answered
5. SEC declares the S-1 Registration Statement "effective"
6. A market maker needs to sponsor the company and file the form 15c2-11 with the NASD (FINRA)
7. Comments from the NASD (FINRA) need to be answered
8. The transfer agent will issue a CUSIP number for the company
9. NASD (FINRA) will assign a ticker symbol for the company
10. The management will do the first trade in accordance with the market maker

Example of business development and milestones for the company

The following 12 months are an example with possible details for a resource company. The company is called ABC Resources, Inc. and is a gold exploration company.

Month 1:

- ABC must complete its corporate audit. The audit will accelerate the submission of regulatory documents
- ABC can then file a S-1 with the SEC
- The S-1 process can take 3-6 months to be approved. ABC must be prepared to act quickly on deficiencies (comment or questions from the SEC)
- CEO and CFO: Register 1,000,000 shares each in S-1 filing
- Seed Shareholders: Register each shareholder's full position in S-1
- ABC should evaluate 2-3 junior gold producers ($5m to $7m buy-in over the next 3 years)
- To achieve market valuations commensurate with ABC's target, a portfolio of 2 to 3 prospective exploration properties and one production asset is required
- Prepare traditional print marketing material

Month 2:

- ABC must stay current with the SEC regarding the S-1 filing
- The key to an accelerated listing is to be aggressive with the SEC. All information must be kept on file with corporate lawyer and ready to be amended (or clarified), then resubmitted as quickly as possible.
- ABC should sign an LOI to acquire or Joint Venture with a junior gold producer
- By the end of month 3, ABC should choose a project and place a cash (&/or share) deposit to secure the asset

Month 3:

- Upon the acquisition of a producing asset, ABC will prepare a financing package
- ABC should finance the acquisition at either $0.85 or $1.00 with a warrant. A new financing package will be drafted; highlighting the S-1 filing, existing assets and the new acquisition. ABC will be eligible for institutional financial support.
- Develop a geological plan 43-101 on project number 1
- ABC should split the cost of a 43-101 technical report on the first property with its joint-venture partner. These reports are mandatory for institutional due diligence.
- Create a German website for European investors
- Commence initial work on the first property (sampling and mapping)

Month 4:

- Develop an email marketing campaign
- ABC will commence an email marketing campaign. The goal is to create an 'opt-in' subscriber base. These emails will not offer securities and must be approved by corporate counsel. The emails will market ABC's assets and management. Prospects will be directed to the website to capture broader profiles.

- Increase the price for the next financing round
- If ABC has moved forward with an asset acquisition, a financing at $0.85 will be attractive to institutional investors. ABC should raise $2 million over the cost of acquisition.
- Maintain aggressive stance with S-1 filing
- Release available data on existing properties
- In month 4, work should have started on project 1 and 2. ABC should release this information (in increments) to existing shareholders and market the information via the email marketing campaign.
- Maintain shareholder database
- In month 4, a corporate communications article should be sent to all shareholders with the request of full correspondence details. The goal is to initiate an up to date database of 2,000 'opt-ins' for further correspondence.
- Create corporate summary Power Point Presentation
- A document that highlights management, projects and finances will be produced in English and German. The document will be available via PDF on the website and will also be used as the core piece of print campaigns.

Month 5:

- Establish a relationship with a Market Maker
- In month 5, ABC should have a clear indication on the status of the S-1 filing. A market maker that will open trading on ABC stock should be selected. The management team should visit the market maker.
- Continue maintaining shareholder database
- The goal is to have complete profiles on 2,000 investors. ABC can accomplish this through consistent communication with its existing shareholders and broader email campaigns (previously described). Further, this activity will instill investor confidence. ABC should plan to send out at least two corporate development emails to shareholders per month.

- ABC should be able to complete financing efforts this month
- Staffing: Once ABC has completed a significant financing (>$3m), a high-profile president with extensive international public company and mining experience should be hired. The president can focus his/her efforts on developing ABC' asset portfolio.
- Establish North American institutional contacts.
- In month 5, a list of the top 20 Canadian and top 30 American finance houses will be identified. A profile of each firm along with a contact in corporate finance will be created.

Month 6:

Turn ABC into a mining company from an exploration company. ABC should aim to be producing and selling gold to generate revenue in the future.

In order to achieve a market valuation in excess of $100m, ABC must be able to support 18-25x P/E ratios. (Example: 25,000,000 share x $4.00 per share = $100 million market capitalization—Earnings: $0.20 per share)

ABC should aim to raise a minimum of $5,000,000 from month 7 to month 18 to support a stock price over $5 per share. Revenue at this level will earn ABC respect in the mining community, international analyst coverage and help ABC meet the listing requirements for NYSE AMEX.

If S-1 has been approved, then file form 15c2-11 with FINRA. This process should take about 2 months and the company will obtain the ticker symbol.

Month 7 to 12:

- Continue email marketing campaign
- Send Corporate Summary to 50 finance houses
- Maintain and enhance shareholder database
- Monitor regulatory file submissions with SEC and maintain audited financial statements
- Open account with Market Maker (cash deposit)
- Establish relationship with German underwriters.
- Collect and review filing requirements for both a Berlin and Frankfurt co-listing.
- Conduct further sampling on exploration properties
- Commence operations with new junior acquisition
- ABC should update shareholders every month. Once again, the goal is to have at least 2,000 shareholder and prospective shareholders ready to participate in trading ABC stock on the public markets.
- Upon OTCBB listing: Instruct Transfer Agent to print unrestricted certificates (in accordance with stock registered via the S-1. Deliver certificates to shareholders.
- Deposit stock with Market Maker.
- Open director and trust accounts at XYZ brokerage firm: deposit stock in each account
- Open individual, corporate and trust accounts at UBS (or other Swiss brokerage firm): deposit stock in each account
- File co-listing documents with Frankfurt and Berlin exchanges.
- Open accounts with German brokerage house and deposit stock.
- Enlist services of Newsletter writers in: Germany, Switzerland, England, USA and Canada.
- ABC will have to budget $5000 per month per newsletter.
- Retain Investor Relations professional (3 month cash & performance contracts) in: Germany, USA and England.
- ABC should budget $10,000 per month and 250,000 options at market value per IR professional.

- In addition, 500,000—1,000,000 free trading shares should be reserved for this operation.
- The most successful promotional tool is direct mail in Europe. The cost is approximately 1 Euro per piece. ABC should budget $400,000 for this program.

Around listing:

- Going forward from this point depends upon SEC and NASD listing approval. If ABC stays on track, an opening price of $1.50 per share is reasonable.
- ABC will have 2-3 exploration properties with current data and a junior producing asset with revenue.
- The new president and the geologists will manage the mining and exploration activities. The CFO will oversee ABC finances and work closely with the accountant and auditor. Former CEO will work directly with financial institutions raising funds to manage international promotion.
- By the end of 24 months, the goal is to be actively traded on 2-3 exchanges, justify a $100m market cap with high quality assets and seek out another acquisition, funded via an offering with a Market Specialist on the NYSE AMEX exchange.
- Develop an exit selling strategy for initial investors

Sample Strategic Plan for the development of an exploration and mining company

The previous plan was focused on the listing process, financing, marketing and initial set-up. The following plan is divided into phases and should give an example of how a company could be developed so that it can increase the number of projects and its valuation. This plan is slightly different but should illustrate how a company could be developed from a business perspective.

Phase 1: Acquisition of initial projects

- Project 1: 100% ownership, located in British Columbia, Canada, early stage development project with geological report and good assays results
- Project 2: Project with about 50,000 oz gold proven and about 500,000 ounces overall potential (Colorado, Mexico, Nevada)

Phase 2: Acquiring the rights for a larger project

- Production play with small upfront investment of $3 million in Mexico
- Securing an option first and then raising capital from institutional clients
- Payback in 2 years of initial investment
- Overall revenue expectancy of $18 million over 5 years
- Additional exploration investment of $2 million to get potential of 700,000 ounces and a fair valuation of at least $100 million

Phase 3: More acquisitions for additional projects to increase project portfolio

- I have access to 4 more projects in Mexico with similar potential to get a total of about 1 to 2 million ounces of gold
- This would put us into a higher league and we could potentially become a takeover target from a mid-tier to larger mining production company

Phase 4: Raising initial capital from private investors

- We have the ability to raise initial capital from my European sales force but their focus is currently on a different deal

- With a public vehicle we could approach groups in Switzerland and smaller gold funds in Switzerland and Liechtenstein

Securing a big project with an option payment

- We have access to 30 to 40 projects each week due to personal relationships in Vancouver.
- Depending on the size and scope of the deal, we might have to come up with larger amounts of money within a few months. To secure a deal of that size it is typical to get a 90-day due diligence period and to make smaller option payment of about $20,000. During this time, we need to organize the money.

Getting financing from institutional investors

- Typically it is very likely to get financing if the following parameters are met:

1. High quality project with real assets (proven reserves)
2. The project has a NI 43-101 report
3. The company is publicly listed—preferably on the TSX (OTC in US has a bad reputation among institutional investors)
4. Good and solid management team (previous successes and reputation)
5. There are only few shares outstanding: 10—30 million and there is a small controllable float

Doing further exploration work—work budget for project

Initial work budget for first project:

- About $10,000 to $20,000
- Sampling, Mapping and Geophysics

Exploration work budget for first project
- About $150,000
- Initial drilling program to drill about 5 holes (discovery drilling)
- NI 43-101 Report can be produced with this budget

Further work programs on other projects

- It makes sense to spend some money on other projects as well to eliminate the bad ones from the good ones
- It is important too, for creating news and not to be dependent on a single project. If the flagship project fails, then the company fails. Therefore it is advisable not to put all eggs into one basket.

Creation of news

- Typically new acquisitions, new directors, new financing rounds but mostly drill results create positive news flow, which is helpful for promoting the stock.

NI 43-101

- In order to get a NI 43-101 (National Instrument— Geological Report with Canadian standards, requirement for listing on TSX) at least CAD$ 100,000 must be spent directly on the project in a 12-month timeframe.
- A certified 43-101 geologist will charge about $30,000 to certify drill results, assay results, etc. and it is comparable to a financial audit
- It does not however say anything about the quality of the project
- It is NOT necessary in the US to have a 43-101 for a listing but it helps to get financing and credibility

Co-listing on TSX Venture Exchange in Canada

- I would strongly advise to consider a co-listing in Canada once the company is further established to attract institutional investors.
- As a former licensed stockbroker in Canada and with relationships to other brokers in Vancouver, it will be simple to get this task done.

Starting operations in Mexico

- Mexico is a very mining friendly country
- I have had a Mexican company in the past and have a trustworthy lawyer and accountant that can be used for operating a project in Mexico.

Work program I: Exploration, Sampling, Mapping and Geophysics

- Typically an initial work program will provide some good usable news results
- The budget for this can range from $10,000 to $50,000 depending on the scope of the project

Work program II: Drilling Phase I—Discovery Drilling (5-10 holes at 200 meters)

- Once some assays have come back from the laboratory with good gold grades (higher than 1 g/T) drilling targets can be identified
- An initial drilling program will cost anywhere from $300,000 to $500,000

Work program III: Drilling Phase II—Target Drilling (25—30 holes)

- Once the initial drill results have come back positive, a second drilling program must be conducted.

- This program will be able to clearly identify a deposit and an average gold grade can determine a number of ounces proven in the ground.
- The budget for this program can range from $1,000,000 to $5,000,000

Feasibility study / Bankable feasibility study

- A feasibility study is the last step before production and will show cost in relation to potential revenue.
- A bankable feasibility study is a guarantee to get financing from a lender to conduct a production. This can range from $20 million to $100 million.

Takeover by a larger mining / production company

- In general it is important to distinguish between an exploration company that is in the business of identifying projects, further advancing existing reserves and putting together an interesting package to be sold off to a mining or production company.
- The business of mining and production is a totally different business model and it can take years to be able to take a project into production and it is normally extremely expensive.
- A mining operation hires a lot of people and there are other kinds of geologists (mining engineers) necessary to complete the task.
- It should be our strategy to build a portfolio of high quality projects, advance them by doing exploration and then to either sell them off or to become a takeover target.
- The only exception I would recommend are those relatively inexpensive production plays in Mexico. This would put the company into a different category (producer) and will generate revenue that will sustain the company on its own without any outside financing. It would also add value and stability to the stock price.

Starting with project 1: $50,000 budget

- Listing project to justify share acquisition and basis for initial round of financing (private investors and smaller gold funds)
- Hiring a geologist for $10,000 to conduct a current geological report

Advancing the early stage project further: $150,000 budget

- 43-101 Report: Minimum amount of money spent on the project (in the ground and on geological work only) is $100,000 in 12 months. $30,000 is the cost for the Report from the geologist. We could take one of our existing exploration projects that seem to have a good potential based on initial sampling and mapping results (budget about $20,000—$30,000) and turn it into a 43-101 certified project. This will give the company a strategic advantage in the financial community to raise capital.

Project 2: Raising $3 million

- Production play in Mexico to put into production and to create a revenue stream in 12 to 24 months. Initial investment: $3 million
- This money needs to come from an institutional investor.

Project 3: Project with proven resources and large upside potential

- Packaging together a series of concessions to create one large deal and spend a few hundred thousand dollars on further advancing the project (estimated exploration budget: $500,000 including acquisition cost of options from landowners) This project will have a multi-million ounce potential and will need major financing in the area of $25 million to put into production. (Colorado projects)

Overall plan:

- We should acquire a portfolio of several projects with different stages in their development ranging from smaller undeveloped exploration projects to production plays. Ideally, we want to secure those deals with an LOI, option agreement or similar with relatively low initial cost. Typically, we will make an option agreement with a smaller payment of $10,000 to $20,000 that will give us the exclusive rights for three months and to do further due diligence on the project. With an agreement in place we have the basis to start soliciting money from institutional clients as we have secured the deal. Ideally, we want to make payments to the landowners on the low end in the beginning and with the majority of the monies to be paid at the back-end of the deal. This is normally in 3 to 4 years.

Increasing valuation from the projects and general valuation methods:

- Even though the gold price is at $1500, you can only take $100 for every ounce of gold proven in the ground as a fair market valuation.
- Additional potential from a project can also be added to the calculation. There are probable resources, indicated resources and proven resources.
- There is not always an exact valuation possible because some of the potential that some projects might have.

Building a real company

- The idea is to start with a smaller and less expensive project to have a foundation to raise capital and it also serves as a listing project.
- There is no NI 43-101 requirement for a listing in the US.

The NI 43-101 Report is a Canadian standard and only required for a TSX listing.

- Based on initial success we can add more projects and increase the quality and scope of the deals.
- We should eventually be focusing on one flagship project but still have other projects for diversification and increased market potential.
- Once we can build up a solid amount of projects, then we should take at least one of them into production once we have the financing in place.
- Once the company is more mature and developed we can either sell it to a larger company, sell some of the projects or find a manager who can run the company and take over.

Achieving a market capitalization of $100 million

- It is not difficult to get a temporary valuation of $100 million if you drive up the price but the main challenge is to justify and being able to sustain this valuation.
- We will need projects with proven reserves that can be expanded. We might be able to get a project with 50,000 ounces proven but with an indicated potential of 500,000 and a possible potential of 1,000,000. All we have to do is to spend money on a drilling program to expand the existing resource.
- If we have a production play like, for example, project 1 in Mexico where we have annual earnings of about $3 million, then we might be able to justify about $30 million in market capitalization with a P/E ratio of 10. But this particular project contains further potential of about 700,000 that would increase the market capitalization if we spend another $2 million in exploration work.

Raising capital by selling shares into market

- A certain percentage of the shares sold in the market

with a marketing campaign should be reinvested into the company to fund and advance the deal.

Example of a pooling agreement:

Key person 1	30%
Key person 2	30%
Key person 3	20%
Company	20%
Total	100%

Other things to consider
- Joint-venture with larger mining group for increasing profile and reputation
- Spin-offs of projects into a separate corporation
- Commence work program to generate news
- PIPE Financing for next acquisition
- Release existing data from project to boost stock
- Increase management profile by hiring new directors with international mining experience
- Increase technical team by hiring additional geologists or having them on the advisory board
- Turn ABC from an exploration and acquisition company into a mining production company
- Establish relationships with German and Swiss underwriters
- Co-listing in Frankfurt
- Mature to NYSE AMEX listed company and fulfill requirements for membership
- Raise capital solely from big institutions to acquire super large deal
- Hire additional management and leave company to new people who will run the business
- Having a tight share structure with very few shares outstanding

- Considering a reverse split to increase the valuation and price
- Creating an exit strategy for initial investors—use them again to fund next deal

Marketing material checklist and other ideas for corporate material

In order to position your company professionally you don't need to have everything covered. The following list should give you some ideas for additional material.

- 2 page flyer overview of company
- Corporate summary document (6 to 10 pages)
- Power Point Presentation as PDF
- Website, Logo and Email
- 1-800 toll free number for telephone and fax
- Share subscription agreement (SSA) in a nice format
- Client information form (CIF) in a nice format
- Private Placement Memorandum (PPM)
- Translation of all documents into a foreign language for local markets (for example German)
- Corporate bank account in USA
- Corporate bank account in Switzerland
- DVD about company and projects
- CD with all documents for someone to complete a full due diligence
- Press articles about the industry and if possible about your company
- Testimonials of happy investors
- 2 page flyer about sales organization / brokerage firm who is selling your deal
- General education and information about the topic of Private Equity
- Sales material for your sales people
- Summary and overview on the process of acquiring shares for new investors

- Explanation on Rule 144 for first time investors
- Complete CVs of all management members
- Technical report and research report or study about project or industry
- Pictures of projects
- Maps and general information about projects
- Brochure about the industry
- Independent analyst report from an independent company to value the company
- Monthly newsletters from the company
- All contracts available in PDF format
- Sample share certificate for new investors

Putting together a management team with "Fallen Angels"

In order to put together an effective management team you will need people who are specialist in a particular field or industry. You will also need people with extensive business background, a good education and relevant business experience. If you are starting out you might feel like no real professional might join your company because you have nothing to show. But that is actually only fear. If you have the fire in you, people will follow you. Also, offer them an advisory board position and give them 20,000 shares annually for being able to use their name. This is very important because you can put together a team of several professionals and it will increase the profile of your deal. I also offered an hourly rate of $100-$150 or $500-$800 per day in case I needed to give them a specific project.

In order to run a successful deal in the beginning, you will need to be in charge and even be the president or CEO of your company. But one person alone doesn't make a management team. You will need other people, too.

There are a lot of good people with great experience out there who can help to make your company a success. But some people are "fallen angels". They used to be successful once but for some reason ended up failing. Some people are 50 years old and they are broke and desperate for money. Something went wrong in their career or life and because of that they will join your team to make money.

Stock Promotion and Marketing

In order to be successful with a company, it will need to be known that the company is public and trading. There are over 13,000 listed companies in the US alone and if no one knows that you exist, no one will buy your shares.

Therefore, it is an important part of your strategy to put aside a certain amount of money for the sole purpose of stock marketing and promotion. I would say that you should have about $500,000 to $1 million in a separate account in the name of a different company available.

This topic is very iffy because of past fraudulent deals and the SEC is keeping a very close eye on the market looking for dodgy deals.

In general, the rule is that for every dollar that you spend on stock marketing, you will generate 3 times of new buying volume if you have a good deal, 5 times of new volume if it is a great deal and even 10 times the volume if you have a fantastic deal with the right connections.

Whether you like it or not, you will have to do a certain amount of promotion. In general, you should do an initial marketing campaign to get things rolling. I would suggest doing a 3-month campaign after you go public to generate new volume and therefore get new investors into your company. I recommend that you will have 2 to 3 news releases each week to get the ball rolling. Try to keep a big acquisition or an important event on hold until you are public. Once you are public this event will help to boost the stock and will be good for you.

The plan should be to sell a certain amount of shares each day into the new volume to turn it into cash.

Example:
Your plan is to sell 1 million shares into the market during the first three months of your company being public. That means that you have to sell about 330,000 shares each month during 22 trading days. This will be about 10,000 to 20,000 shares per day.

If your goal is to list your company at $0.50 per share and then to drive the price up to about $2.00, you should have an average selling price of about $1.00 per share sold.

In order for you to make one million in three months, you will have to sell one million shares at an average price of $1.00. This is very possible and realistic without hurting the company or the share price.

You will have to balance and sell carefully into new volume so that you don't hurt the stock price and bring it down by selling your own position. You should sell more on a lot of volume and sell less on little volume. The goal is to keep the share price positive and going up while selling off some of your shares to turn them into cash.

Sometimes your volume and the market can react really well and you can sell 30 million or more in three months and sometimes it is very difficult and you won't be able to sell much.

The more marketing funds you have available and the better you do your promotion, the more shares can you turn into cash.

Exit strategy for your investors

Be aware that your investors trusted you in the beginning when you had nothing to show for it and you needed the money to get going. Therefore you should create an exit strategy for your investors so that they make money, too. Once you have created a successful exit for your investors and they made money with it, they will trust you even more and will automatically reinvest into your next deal.

This is very true because when I did my first deal and the people made money, over 80% of all investors invested into my second deal and invested even more money than the first time around.

If you have a pool of happy investors you can use them over and over again for future deals. This alone will give you financial power, stability, influence and leverage. You will never ever have to worry about the future again. But keep in mind that you are only as successful as you last deal.

Investor relations and promotion

What is stock promotion? Once a company is listed on an exchange you can initiate a promotion program to make your stock more known. The goal is to create a lot of attention so that new investors will buy your stock via their broker. This will create a lot of volume in your title.

Without any new buyers your stock will not be actively traded and nothing happens.

There is no point in having a public company if no one knows that it exists. There are over 13,000 listed companies in the US and you need to do something that brokers and investors will be attracted to your title.

There are a number of marketing strategies that you can use to create market awareness. Things like newsletters to potential investors, research reports or online presence in stock portals are just a few to mention.

The main goal of a promotional program is to sell your or the company's shares. Typically, a company hires a promoter that is the only person with free trading shares. The promoter has for example 10 million shares available and initiates a marketing program. Usually, he has a lot of contacts of potential buyers or lists of people that are interested in buying new issues. He puts the company in the best light possible and sends out marketing material to those potential buyers. The buyers get interested and put in orders through their brokers to buy your shares. Since you or the promoters are the only people who are sellers you sell your positions to new investors.

Other marketing methods:

- Email marketing
- Physical mailers
- Print ads in industry related magazines
- Call rooms

Basics for a successful promotional campaign

In order for a promotional stock marketing campaign to be successful a number of factors need to be in place:

Factor 1: Control over the float of the free-trading shares

The number one rule to make a campaign successful is that one party controls most of the free-trading shares. Only if there is a structured selling of the shares can it be made sure that the price won't get hurt and that the stock can go in the desired direction.

If all of your investors have free trading shares right when the company goes public, some of them will want to sell immediately which will make it harder for you to keep your share price up. That is why I always have a clause in the share subscription agreement that all investors have at least 6 to 12 months of an additional holding period or selling restriction in addition to Rule 144 once the first day of trading happens. I have had to learn that lesson the hard way with Hemis. Hemis was doing really well when it went public but because I gave all investors free trading shares because I thought I was being nice and fair, some people started selling their positions and eventually it put too much pressure on the stock price that it gradually went down. It created a downward spiral that eventually became unstoppable. In the end it killed the deal and my reputation. If no one was able to sell for 12 months after the IPO the company could have had some time to further develop its business model and create a share price that was more stable.

Factor 2: Right share structure

You can go public but if you don't have enough free trading paper (shares) you won't be able to sell them into the market and turn them into cash. That is why it is important right from the start when you first set up your company that you plan for the promotional campaign. You need to have at least 10 to 20 million shares available for promotion. If you hire a promoter or a group they will require a few million shares for themselves so that they can make money. If you only have 1 or 2 million shares available for them, they won't be interested in taking on your deal. If they use all their contacts and marketing methods, they usually expect to get sell all of the 20 million shares over the course of 3 months. If they only have one million shares, it won't be worth it for them.

It is easier to issue shares right from the start at par value ($0.00001) and assign them to a few corporations that are your strategic positions. The goal is to have share positions that have less than 5% of the outstanding shares. So if you have 50 million shares outstanding, you should have less than 2.5 million shares per company as a strategic trading position. Ideally you want to have 4.9%

You also have to make sure that you don't issue too many shares so that you won't have any problems with dilution or the valuation later. You can always cancel shares once you have issued too many. That won't cost you anything. But it looks really bad if you have to issue 2.5 million shares for some kind of services once your stock price is already at $1.00 per share. It looks obviously bad on your financial statements and everybody will figure out what you are trying to do right away.

Factor 3: Marketability of the company

If you don't have a "sexy story" it will be hard to promote your deal. Sometimes it is better to wait if your industry is not in high demand. Your deal should be right for the market and should be unique with its main selling slogan.

Factor 4: Fundamentals

You can promote companies for a few months that have absolutely no assets and push the stock higher. But eventually, a deal like that will always collapse.

It is much better to have a solid business model and assets in the company for the long run. If you do have a good and solid company, it will sooner or later work out for everybody.

Factor 5: News Releases

Every campaign needs about 2 to 3 news releases per week. If you plan on doing a promotional campaign for 3 months you will have to prepare your news releases in advance.

According to US securities law you need to file an 8-K with the SEC (current report) within 4 days of any important event happening. That means that you should wait strategically with things like acquisitions, work programs, results, new management members, etc. until you start your campaign. You can defer some events into the future but you already know that you are going to implement them into your company.

Factor 6: All free trading shares must be with one broker

You can have the best deal but if one person in your group doesn't play by the rules and decides to sell some shares secretly through his own account, your deal might be in jeopardy. Because of uncontrolled selling it might be hard to control and stabilize the share price. That is why I suggest having all accounts with one broker and brokerage firm when doing a promotion. The only kind of selling will come from this broker and you will know and be able to find out if there is someone trying to mess with your deal.

Some campaigns have two groups working on a deal and if both groups work against each other by selling uncontrollably into the market, it might actually hurt the deal instead of helping it.

Daily plan of a promotion

Trading starts at 10 am and stops at 4 pm Eastern Time. It is often important to have a good closing price compared to the previous day. Sometimes it is better to sell less shares into the market and even to buy back shares to get the price back up to an acceptable level again.

Typically, there will be more volume on days when a news release comes out. On those days you should be prepared to sell off more shares than on regular days.

Time frame of a promotion

Normally, a promotion is between two and three months long. The goal is to sell as many shares during this time as possible. If a promoter sells 30 million shares in 3 months, the company should be aware that sooner or later those 30 million shares will come against it one day. One day those people who have bought those shares will eventually sell their positions again. So if the promoter was able to increase the price from $1.00 to $5.00 in those three months, it is very likely that by too many people selling it will come back to $1.00 one day.

Paying a promoter

A promoter or a group is almost never interested in the long success of the company. All they care about is how many shares they can get rid of (or sell into the market) and turn them into cash. Promoters are sharks and you cannot trust them. Some promoters will get 80% of all proceeds or 10 million shares but they will sell what they can to make money for themselves first and not worry about your positions.

It is a very delicate matter if you decide to hire a group. There are so many mistakes that you can make. Believe me, I made them all and paid dearly for it.

You need to decide whether you want to hire a group or organize it yourself. You will often have much more volume and selling power with a strong group but the problem might be that your company will fail afterwards because of too much selling pressure. If your company is dependent on outside capital and it is important that the share price is at a stable level you should consider waiting with the campaign and focus more on developing your company.

It is often also more advisable to pay people like newsletter writers or other marketing related services in cash instead of stocks. Because once these people have shares, they will sell them without consideration for your plans. It is better to have a budget set aside for promotion that you were able to build before you go public to protect the company later.

A friend of mine was involved in a deal were he had to pay 90% to the promoters. But this group was so powerful that in one week, they created a volume of 35 million shares at about $0.40 per share. In one day alone during the following week, they generated a volume of 20 million shares for $0.40, which is about $8 million. My friend made only 10% but it was $800,000 in one day! Not bad I would say . . .

The right share structure

In general, there is no right or wrong share structure. However, depending on your strategy you will have to decide how you want to have your company structured when it comes to promotion. You could decide to have 50 million shares outstanding in total and start with a price of $1.00 per share or you could have 250 million shares and start out at $0.20 per share. Your plan could be to sell a lot more shares below a dollar just to create the volume that you like.

In most cases you will want to have, for example, 10 corporations (ideally offshore from Europe or from an island like Panama or Marshall Islands, etc.) with each holding a share position of 4.9% of the total outstanding shares. You could have 10 positions holding 2.4 million shares each and therefore have a total of 24 million shares available. Each one of those companies needs to have a different beneficial owner. In fact, it must be 10 of your close friends or people that you can trust who are willing to give their name to officially own a corporation. All of those offshore companies and their positions should have accounts outside of the US.

If you are doing a promotion in Germany there are different rules. It is much easier there because you can decide which shares will be free trading and which shares should be restricted. By co-listing a company in Frankfurt, which is very easy and quick once you have a ticker symbol in the US, you might be able to run your promotion in Europe rather than in the US.

Pooling Agreement

This is another delicate topic. It is not legal in the US to create a pooling agreement to sell shares as a group of several individuals. In Germany on the other hand, it is legal. But if you don't organize yourself in a similar manner, your deal will get screwed up because there will be uncontrolled selling and greed from your own team members. It is human nature and very hard to avoid.

A pooling agreement is a contract that is being done by a lawyer. It describes the percentage and share positions of the most important shareholders and the promoter. The main idea is that every time shares are being sold from the main account, that it will be distributed according to a key that was defined in advance. Here is an example:

35%	promoter
15%	shareholder 1
12%	shareholder 2
10%	shareholder 3
10%	shareholder 4
8%	shareholder 5
5%	shareholder 6
5%	shareholder 7
100%	8 parties

If one million shares were sold at an average price of $2.00 per share, then the proceeds would be $2 million. 35% or $700,000 would go into the account for the promoter and shareholder 3 with 10% would get $200,000. Typically, you would do those transactions every day at the end of the business day.

Problems and danger of a bad promotion and organization

The worst for any promotional campaign is uncontrolled selling. Because of uncontrolled selling the price gets under pressure and starts to fall. Eventually, there will be a downward spiral that is hard to stop. At that point everybody will lose faith and external short sellers will start to short your stock and make it worse.

Another thing that can go wrong is bad timing or loss of time due to an administrational mistake. This can cost the campaign a lot of money. If the original plan was to initiate several marketing activities in a predefined manner and a couple of them fail, the efficiency of the campaign will suffer.

Also, if your campaign is under-financed it can also lead to a devastating end.

The attractiveness and timing of your industry also plays a huge importance. If your deal is out of fashion it will be very hard to motivate new investors to get in. On the other hand if your deal's timing in regards to the current trends and popularity are good, then deals with little substance can do really well.

The main thing is that one person is watching the entire promotion like a hawk. There are so many things that can go wrong because everything is sensitive. A good preparation is key.

Preparation pre-IPO / marketing before the company is public

A company that is not yet listed typically has a number of different marketing materials like a website, flyers, brochures, investors' package and maybe even a video.

In most cases it can be helpful to wait with making the IPO a publicly known event. If you are quoting a new start-up company it is actually a very quiet event. No one really knows the ticker symbol and the first day of trading is normally only done by the people involved. Most of the time, existing investors don't even realize that the company is already listed. Since most investors will have restricted stocks it is better that way anyway because you will get a lot of phone calls of people who want to sell faster.

A marketing program before a listing is not necessary unless you have a well-known company. It is important that you have a good start in the first week. Once you start launching your marketing activities, the volume will increase and the attention will be on your stock.

Investor Relations

It can be very helpful to hire an investor relations group for a few months. Since you will be trading and busy with other things, this group can deal with your small investors, answer any questions that they might have, deal with difficult people, motivate them to hold on to their position and send out material to new potential clients. A service like that can cost about $5000 per month but it can save you a lot of time and headaches. As the main initiator or management member this will be the busiest time for you.

News Releases

News releases are the most important part of a campaign because it helps to create volume. Ideally, you want to release 2 to 3 news releases during a campaign per week.

Often news releases are purposely withheld for a certain period of time and timed to be released when a marketing activity will take place. The combination of a great news release with the right marketing activity can create a lot of new buying volume.

Typically, news releases will be written in such a manner that they actually sound better than the event is in reality. You cannot lie and it has to be fact based but you can spin it in a manner that it seems to have more importance to the overall development and future of the company.

Just to release a news release without combining it with a marketing activity is a waste of time and money because it won't create volume.

There are several ways to make a news release. You can either file an 8-K (current report) with the SEC and describe very dry and facts oriented what the change is all about or you can use an Internet based company like for example www.prnewswire.com to publish them.

Research Report

It helps to get an independent research report from an analyst or a company. This report should show and explain the potential of the company and give a higher price recommendation to potential investors.

Typically, investment companies analyze big corporations and do their research and then publish a report. But if you are a small start-up company you can also secretly hire and pay for this service. Most companies do that. The more reputable the company is where it is coming from the more credible is the report.

The main goal is to create an additional marketing tool that makes the company look good.

Opening price

An initial price is very important. The number of issued and outstanding shares multiplied by the share price equals the value of the company or the market capitalization. So if you have 50 million shares issued and your opening price is at $1.00 then your company is valued at $50 million. Now the question is whether this valuation is justified and if it still has potential in your price to grow. Ideally, you want to start out with rather a lower price so that new investors will be motivated to get in. But if you set the price too high, let's say at $2.00 per share your valuation might all of a sudden be too high and therefore the only way for your stock is downwards.

Studies have shown that stocks under $1.00 will be traded more frequently than higher priced stocks. The reason for this is because most investors will only be able to invest a few thousand dollars and psychologically they get a larger amount of shares if they have a cheaper priced stock.

After you have filed the form 15c2-11 with FINRA through your market maker you will also get a price range that was approved by FINRA to get your first quote. Typically, the first price will not be too far away from your last round of financing. But it is the discretion of the company and the market maker where you want to have your first trade.

Normally, your market maker will have a certain amount of shares of your company and he will place a selling order into the system. Your job is to place a buying order for the same price and amount into the system through your brokerage account and the first trade will take place.

Pump and Dump

Pump and dump is a term that is often misused. It describes creating volume to increase the price of a stock of a company who has very little value or assets. The volume that is created is based not based on facts and real value but only based on hype. Some stocks will trade from $1.00 to $10.00 in a few weeks by the millions and once the promotional campaign is over and everybody is selling their position, the price will rapidly drop back or even below $1.00. The whole process and the increase were not based on actual positive developments of the company but on hype and promotion.

Pump and dump is illegal and it is the main reason why people go to jail when it comes to public markets. The SEC has systems in place that observe these kinds of activities automatically and if you have become a target of their investigation, everything will be scrutinized. Therefore, you must be really careful if your stock price goes up too fast for no real reason. Often it is better to bring it down to a reasonable level yourself to avoid any kind of suspicion.

Creating an exit strategy for your investors

In the perfect world you want to create an exit strategy for your initial investors so that you can use them again for future deals.

But taking on such a big responsibility might not be in the best interest of your company and every investor invested their money knowing about the risks and that they can lose their investment. It was their choice to invest and not yours.

Going public and being able to sell shares into the open market IS the exit strategy for someone who has bought shares of a private company. The only question is whether the investor is able to sell the shares for a higher price and if he can get rid of his position when there is sufficient volume in the market. Some projects do well but the main problem is the volume. If someone bought 100,000 shares pre-IPO he might not be able to sell all of his shares in one transaction and for the same price.

Therefore, I suggest that you try to plan your promotional efforts in such a way that there is going to be enough volume available to get your initial investors out of the deal so that they don't lose any money. Example: If you were able to raise $2.5 million at $0.50 per share and issued 5 million shares for your investors and your plan is to sell off 20 million shares in your promotional campaign, then your goal should be to make less money for yourself and to use part of the proceeds to buy back the shares of your investors.

There is absolutely no obligation for you to do so and you are basically giving away money but it is the right and the smart thing to do. If you are able to make sure that your investors don't lose money and even make a small profit, you will have their trust and 80% of the investors will reinvest their money into your deal venture—often, with more money that they invested in the first place.

When I bought back about $2 million from the initial investors of Hemis, I gave them back their initial investment and let them keep half of their shares. I basically bought half of their share position for double the price. Everybody was happy and some of them were able to sell the rest for an even higher price in the market. The consequence was that when I initiated my second deal that 80% reinvested without any questions and I even received orders by fax and by email without having talked to them.

When I was a broker in Canada there was a deal called Wolfden Resources. Wolfden was a huge success in the first year and when the same group launched their second project, they got all the funding that they ever needed. All that people said was: "Hey, this deal is being organized by the same group that did Wolfden." After that statement, no more questions were necessary.

So the moral is that you are only as good as your last deal and if your reputation gets damaged it is very hard to recover from it.

Interaction between company and promotion

Legally, the company is not allowed to do any kind of promotion. The money that is being used for marketing and promotion cannot come from the company. Depending on the laws of a country the company could get into trouble for market manipulation. That is why the promotional team has to be a separate group.

Controlling the price

Again, legally you are not allowed to control, manipulate or influence the stock price. In reality however, if you control the majority of the free trading shares you will have a certain amount of control over the development of the stock price. This is the case for at least the beginning. After a while once too many shares have been sold into the market, it is almost impossible to control it anymore.

The only thing that a company can do is to wait for the last 5 minutes of the trading day and try to place an order to get a high closing price or to avoid a disastrous low price.

In general, a stock price will go up if there are more buying than selling orders in the system.

Bid support

When you look at a stock price you can see the ASK and BID price. Professional traders will check out the Nasdaq Level II System and see how many orders are on each side. This will show how strong the support of a certain price level is.

One strategy is to have an account with for example $100,000 ready and put create the bid support for a stock. If you can see that too many selling orders are hurting the price you can use that money to create stability by buying your own stock back. This will prevent the price from falling too much. Once again, this is technically not legal in the US but most promoters are doing it anyway.

Advancing your company to the next level

No matter what kind of marketing campaign you are planning, the best way to get ahead is to create a real company with real results. The goal is to raise money to further advance the company's projects and to financially strengthen the company so that it can expand, make the necessary acquisitions and increase its assets.

Money raising for a public company

Companies always require new capital. Once a company is public it can do a PIPE financing. PIPE stands for Private Placement into a Public Entity. If the current stock price is at $2.00 per share, the company could make an offer to issue shares at $1.20 but with a 6-month selling restriction (Rule 144). This offer is below market price and attractive for investors and it will bring new money into the company.

The cost of a promotional campaign

The cost can vary greatly. A small promotion could be organized for $500,000 and a larger promotion for $5 million. It really depends on the kind of activities that you are planning. Sometimes a group has the budget already available before they launch their deal but mostly they finance the ongoing costs each week by financing it through the sale of stock. A typical campaign can cost anywhere between $50,000 to $250,000 per week.

I personally know a Chinese newsletter writer who charges $10,000 per day for his email marketing efforts. That seems to be a lot of money at first but he guarantees at least $50,000 in new buying volume.

It is very hard to say what is working efficiently during the time that you read this book. Things are constantly changing and some newsletter writers are successful in one deal and then horrible in the next. Again: people are only as successful as their last deal.

Earning potential of a successful campaign

I have seen many successful campaigns. People with average intelligence but with the right connections can literally make millions of dollars in a few weeks and months. I have met a promoter who was 26 years old from Austria who made at least $10 million every three months while he was promoting a deal.

Let's do an example: You start out at $1.00 per share and you were able to bring the price up to a level of $2.00 while selling 30 million shares in 3 months. Let's assume that your average price was $1.50 per share. In that case you or your group made $45 million!

This example shows you that it can totally be worth it to get into this field. But the problem could also be that you put up a couple of million dollars to launch a deal, spend all the money and make zero because your deal failed.

The main goal should be to create enough capital for the company so that it will be more stable and that it will have enough funds even after the promotion to continue its business activities. You also need to be very careful not to violate any securities laws and to avoid any kind of lawsuits from investors who have lost money in the process.

Ethical concerns

Promoters are all sharks. 95% of them are crooks and only have their own interest in mind. They promise you the world but the end result often leads to disaster.

A lot of promoters sell their own share position first and when it comes to selling shares for you or the company, they abandon the deal and cease their efforts. Often they create more damage for a company than benefits.

Another critical factor is the legal side. Promoters often work in the grey areas of the law. They do things to create market awareness that are not 100% legal.

Choosing a promoter is critical for your future. It can break you and destroy your reputation. My advice is that you don't hire a promoter at all. Work on the company and do your own campaign. Use the marketing methods that I have described in this program and stay 100% legal. You might not make as much money but you will be better off in the long run. The only person who should control campaign is you.

Actual companies and ideas for a campaign

<u>Canada</u>

- Stockgroup (Vancouver) $5,000 per month
- Skyline (Ottawa) $10,000 per month
- Renmark (Montreal) $5,000 per month

Europe (Germany)

Research:	
Global-smallcap-report	One of the leading independent research-labels specialized on small-caps
Schmider Investments	Well known label in small cap-market
Performaxx	Independent research label with biggest subscriber-base in Germany
Frankfurter Finance	Independent research label
eMail-Newsletter	
	Production costs for an editorial html-newsletter
aktiencheck.de	Leading supplier of summaries of stock-reports
Finanzen & Börse	One of the best performing stock newsletters in Germany (new subscribers only)
Performaxx	Independent research label with one of the biggest
ariva.de	one of the biggest websites for growth stocks (former new market)
boerse.de	General interest stock-portal with well-known domain-name (German: exchange.de)
Frankfurter Finance	Independent research label with own subscriber-base
smallcap-investor	Stock newsletter with one of the biggest subscriber-bases
Trade & win	Stock newsletter
Boerse go	Financial website and stock newsletter specialized on traders and tec-analysis
Der Aktionaer	Leading financial print-magazine (editorial ad including production costs)
aktienmarkt.de	Supplier of stock-newsletter with summaries of stock-reports
Small-cap-news	Independent research-label specialized on small caps with own subscriber-base
Boerse-inside	Stock newsletter specialized on small caps with big impact

Print-magazines	
	Production costs for an editorial ad in all magazines (different dates means updates)
Der Aktionaer	Leading financial print-magazine specialized on stocks
Euro am Sonntag	Leading financial newspaper in Germany
Focus money	Leading financial magazine for general money interest

Internet portals in Germany (www . . .)

- Ariva.de
- Aktienmarkt.net
- Aktieninformation.de
- Biotech-world.de
- Bloomberg
- Boerse-go.de
- Boerse-online.de
- Capital.de
- Cortalconsors.de
- Equitystory.com
- Finanzen.net
- Goingpublic.de
- Handelsblatt.de
- Impulse.de
- More-ir.de
- Onvista.de
- Platow.de
- Smartinvestor.de
- Tradecross.de
- Wallstreet-online.de
- Wirtschaftswoche.de

Example of a media budget for Germany from the past

Label:	Description:	Subscriber-base:	cpt:	A piece:	Pieces:	Price
	Publication of all news regarding via aktiencheck newsfeed (monthly fee)			1,500 €	5	7,500 €
	Publication of all recommendations via aktiencheck-research feed			1,500 €	5	7,500 €
Research:						
Global-small cap-report	One of the leading independent research-labels specialized on small-caps			2,500 €	3	7,500 €
Schmider Investments	Well known label in small cap-market			3,000 €	3	9,000 €
Performaxx	Independent research label with biggest subscriber-base in Germany			4,000 €	3	12,000 €
Frankfurter Finance	Independent research label			3,500 €	3	10,500 €
Email-Newsletter						
	Production costs for an editorial html-newsletter			1,000 €	6	6,000 €
aktiencheck.de	Leading supplier of summaries of stock-reports	112,000	45 €	5,000 €	6	30,000 €
Finanzen & Börse	One of the best performing stock newsletters in Germany (new subscribers only)	80,000	75 €	6,000 €	6	36,000 €
Performaxx	Independent research label with one of the biggest	275,000	16 €	4,275 €	6	25,650 €
ariva.de	One of the biggest websites for growth stocks (former new market)	40,000	100 €	4,000 €	6	24,000 €

boerse.de	General interest stock-portal with well-known domain-name (German: exchange.de)	38,000	72 €	2,750 €	6	16,500 €
Frankfurter Finance	Independent research label with own subscriber-base	60,000	67 €	4,000 €	6	24,000 €
Smallcap-investor	Stock newsletter with one of the biggest subscriber-bases	140,000	36 €	5,000 €	6	30,000 €
trade & win	Stock newsletter	70,000	40 €	2,800 €	6	16,800 €
Boerse go	Financial website and stock newsletter specialized on traders and technical analysis	43,000	60 €	2,580 €	6	15,480 €
Der Aktionaer	leading financial print-magazine (editorial ad including production costs)	90,000	78 €	7,000 €	6	42,000 €
aktienmarkt.de	Supplier of stock-newsletter with summaries of stock-reports	47,000	70 €	3,290 €	6	19,740 €
small-cap-news	Independent research-label specialized on small caps with own subscriber-base	68,000	37 €	2,500 €	6	15,000 €
boerse-inside	Stock newsletter specialized on small caps with big impact	90,000	111 €	10,000 €	6	60,000 €
Print-magazines						
	Production costs for an editorial ad in all magazines (different dates means updates)			2,500 €	6	15,000 €
Der Aktionaer	Leading financial print-magazine specialized on stocks	90,000	75 €	6,750 €	6	40,500 €
Euro am Sonntag	Leading financial newspaper in Germany	109,000	101 €	11,016 €	6	66,096 €
Focus money	Leading financial magazine for general money interest	139,485	95 €	13,300 €	6	79,800 €
Total:						**616,566 €**

Additional marketing activities and ideas

- Email marketing (paid addresses)
- Email Marketing (own list)
- Physical mailer or brochure
- Newsletter (own list)
- Newsletter (paid addresses)
- Research Report (independent report)
- Research Report (own report)
- Call center
- Giving presentations at brokerage houses
- Sending out letters to brokers and finance houses
- Developing a list of European contacts
- Newsletter strategy: Recommend 3 good deals first (not your own) and then recommend your deal right after
- Videos
- TV Spots
- Markus Frick Shows (Finance Guru in Germany)
- PR news articles
- Gather names of other shareholder lists

Attitude is everything—36 secrets of success

Secret 1: Everything is possible for you in this life

No matter where you come from or what you have done so far in your life, you can have, be or do anything.

The only thing that matters is the thing that you want most in this life. If you want something more than anything else and you never give up, you will eventually end up with your desired goal.

There is absolutely nothing that you cannot do, have or be. You might have to work a lifetime on achieving your goal and never give up. But there is nothing that you cannot do that others have done before you.

You might have to get advice from others that have done what you would like to do, read all the books that are available, keep trying and trying until you succeed and keep improving your skills and knowledge along the way.

If you keep learning, you will eventually get there.

Life is like a tennis game. You might be behind and seem to be losing with a current result of 0-6 / 0-6 / 0-5 and 0-40 but you can still win the game! That is the great thing about tennis. No matter how badly you have done you can win the game at any point in time. And the same is true for your life!

You can do anything! It might not be easy and requires work but anything is possible!
The only thing holding you back is your own doubt in your own abilities.

Secret 2: You don't need anybody's approval

Often people worry too much about what others might say or think. Some people are so extremely focused on the approval from others that they don't dare to follow their dreams.

Sometimes it is best to simply leave all the worries behind and just do it! Don't think of what others might think or what kind of consequences it might have. As long as you don't hurt anybody else, there is nothing that you shouldn't do.

Being free from fear is very liberating. Sometimes doing something silly or risky can make you happy. Some people feel trapped in an invisible prison that society set for them. Often people also make made their own prison.

If you have a business idea but you have concerns, then do it anyway. Just do it!

If you don't try things, you will never know if it works. Sometimes doing or trying things will give you insights that you would not get if you didn't do it in the first place.

Just be active and do things! You will figure out along the way what is right for you and what is not.

Secret 3: You need momentum in the beginning

Some people call themselves perfectionists. The problem with trying to do things perfectly all the time is that most people don't even get started, take forever to finish a task, cannot make a decision, are not satisfied with the result and end up giving up frustrated.

When people start a new business, they most often lack money. They cannot afford to hire professionals to help them with their business or marketing.

The trick is to do things in the beginning that are 80% perfect and acceptable but could still be improved in the future.

This is how I used to write my brochures or marketing material. I didn't worry too much about making it perfectly because then I would have lost momentum.

It is extremely important that you keep your momentum and finish things fast in the beginning. Just get the job done now and improve your sales material or presentation later in the future.

You might not get all the clients yet that you want but you will get a few and that is important to get you going.

Once you have gotten results, you can improve your business. You need to start with what you have right now and do what you can right now. In a later stage, money and other resources will come.

You need to focus on getting the first few sales in. This will motivate you to keep going.

If you lack money or other things then do now what you can with the things that are available today. There is nothing else now! If you really do what you can with what you have, you will have done your best.

Secret 4: Start small, finish big

Even if you don't have much money in the beginning you can get started. Acquire an option for your first project or product. If you are smart, you might even be able to get an option for no money down. Get your first project and realize that it is just the beginning. More and better projects will follow as you can raise more capital.

Getting started is often the key to success.

Secret 5: Clarity is power

One of the most important things, if not the most important thing, in achieving any goal is clarity. You need to know exactly what it is to the last detail in order to get it. If you say, for example, that you want to be rich and have lots of money, then you will not achieve anything.

A goal is something measurable and has a timeline for its achievement. Otherwise it is merely a wish without any future.

People with goals are successful because they know in which direction they need to go. That is the whole secret. Most people have no goals or fuzzy goals that don't serve them.

The world is an interesting place. Everything is available in abundance. There is money like sand on the beach. There is absolutely every imaginable thing out there. The only question is why you don't have it already.

You need to understand that life is like a food buffet. You can have anything you want but you need to know what it is exactly that you would like to have. Only then you will be able to get it.

You give your order to the universe by making a list and dwelling on each individual goal each day. All your actions should have something to do with the attainment of your goals.

> People who plan are four times as successful
> as people who don't plan.
> (Bill Phillips, founder of EAS Nutrition)

Secret 6: Salami technique—making a big project small and manageable

> Nothing is really hard when you break it down into little steps.

Trying to eat a huge salami in one attempt is almost impossible. If you cut off thin little slices and eat them one at a time, you will eventually have eaten the whole salami. That is what I call the salami technique. Each day you cut off a thin slice and eat it.

When it comes to achieving a big goal, you also need to apply the salami technique. You write down the big goal and then divide it into small little steps and tasks that can be done on a daily basis. The more you break down your goal into little steps the easier will it appear.

When you think about it, there is nothing really difficult to achieve. It might just be a hundred little steps until you reach your goal.

Don't ever get intimidated by big goals. You can reach any goal if you apply the salami technique and if the goal is worth the effort.

Basically, it all comes down to planning. Start with the end goal and work your way backwards.

Secret 7: He without fear is king of the world

Most people are paralyzed by fear. Because of that they play things safe in life and never do anything out of the ordinary.

If you keep doing what the masses are doing you will have what everybody else has: nothing. You will be dependent on the state and you will keep struggling financially.

In order to have something different, you need to do something different. You need to be brave and courageous in your actions and do the things that most people are afraid of.

To be afraid is normal. Everybody is afraid from time to time. The idea is not to get rid of the fear realize that you are afraid and do it anyway. Fear is your biggest enemy. You are your own biggest enemy.

People are two basic fears: Fear of failure and fear of rejection. In business you need to create sales. Obviously, not everybody is going to like what you have to offer. Therefore lots of people will reject you and your products.

A lot of things might seem out of your league or far away. But you might be surprised what is possible if you act courageously. If you do things despite your fears or worries, there is no limit to what you can achieve.

Secret 8: Self-confidence is the most important thing for success

If you don't believe in yourself, you cannot expect others to believe in you.

Self-confidence is the single most important factor for success. It is the one quality and characteristic that all successful people have in common. It is the foundation of all achievements and the level of self-confidence of successful people is greater than the one of an ordinary person.

Your future is unlimited when you believe in yourself.

Ask yourself the following questions: What one thing would you dare to dream if you knew you could not fail? If you were completely unafraid of anyone or anything and you felt completely free to act in any area?

Only fear and doubt in your own abilities is holding you back. With greater self-confidence in yourself you will set bigger goals, bigger plans and commit to achieving objectives that today you only dream about. You will take whatever steps are necessary to earn more money and to enjoy a better lifestyle. You would do what you really want to do and you refuse to conform to the wishes or opinions of anyone else. With greater self-confidence you would be bolder and more imaginative. You would commit yourself to projects that today are only sitting on the backburner of your mind. You would feel simply invincible. You will feel a tremendous sense of control, which is the foundation of happiness, well-being and success. You will feel like the master of your fate and in charge of your life.

Secret 9: Don't give away your power by blaming other people and circumstances

People tend to blame other people or circumstances for their failures. The truth is that you are responsible for everything that happens to you. Once you stop blaming others and take full responsibility you will realize that it is only you who can shape your destiny.

Even if something happened to you that at first you feel like you had no control over and because of that you did not achieve your goal, you need to stop blaming the circumstances or people involved.

You need to realize that it was because of lack of planning on your side or not judging the situation correctly. Once you take full responsibility and stop giving away blame, you free yourself from the helplessness that comes with failure.

Some people intentionally try to take advantage of you and in the end you might lose something. It is not the other person that you should blame—you should blame only yourself. You did not judge the situation right or you ignored the little signs. You did not prepare or protect yourself enough in case things did not go as originally planned. You were a poor judge of character or you were disillusioning yourself from the potential promises that came with the situation.

You should always have a plan B and assume that your plan will not work perfectly. You should always think strategically like a chess player and prepare yourself for any deviation of the plan that might occur. Once you stop dreaming about the outcome and take full control of what needs to be done, you stop being unrealistic and start getting control of your plan.

No one is to blame but you in case something doesn't go according to plan. Surely, people and circumstances can make your life harder but in the end it is your responsibility and no one else's whether or not you achieve your goals. Bad people and unfortunate situations are merely a normal occurrence or disturbance in any undertaking. No plan is ever working as originally thought of. There will always be unexpected situations. That is just a part of life.

So from now on you need to stop blaming others because then you give away control over your own happiness. If you give away control, then someone else or simply chance will determine what happens to you.

Secret 10: No one will do it for you

Young girls dream about a prince that will come one day and save them. Others hope that someone will see their potential and give them a chance. And again others hope that they will come across some sort of lucky situation that will make them rich over night.

The hard truth is that no one is coming to the rescue. No matter how good you might be as a person on the inside and no matter what your intensions might be you cannot expect to be saved.

If you want to achieve anything, you need to do the necessary steps yourself. No one will do it for you. No one will work for you for free. No one will give you anything just because of the greatness of his or her heart. The only exceptions are your parents and the people that love you.

But even the people that love you can only do so much. There is a limit to what they will do for you and they need to deal with their own life and problems.

If you want anything above the ordinary, you need to do it yourself. You need to stop dreaming and start planning real steps on paper. You need to determine exactly what it is that you want and make a detailed plan for its achievement.

You should always ask yourself whether you really are realistic with a situation or whether you hope that certain things will just be. Once you are truly honest with yourself and you realize that some factors of a situation are merely wishes on your part and the chance of actually happening seem unrealistic. This is a very difficult step for many people. But once you are able to look at every situation from a distance with a hard and realistic view, you will start changing the outcome of a situation and move forward positively.

Secret 11: Laziness will kill all dreams

> Laziness will eventually cause you more
> pain than working hard now.

Most people work eight hours per day and while they are at work, they spend a lot of time with tasks that waste time. These are things like chatting with co-workers, taking extended coffee breaks, surfing the Internet and so on.

If you work, you should work. When it is your free time, then you should enjoy it and not work. But when you are in your office then you should fully focus your attention on working and achieving your goals.

Sometimes working twelve instead of eight hours will make a huge difference in where you will end up. Think about all the time-wasting activities you do on a daily basis that doesn't really get you ahead. One for example is watching TV. The average person watches three to four hours of TV each day.

Working harder and longer has a potential effect that will improve your results not only by the hours that you put in but will multiply the end result.

Secret 12: Self-discipline is inevitable for any success

> People who are successful are all without exception highly self-disciplined.

So if you want to be successful you need to develop the habit of self-discipline. There is no two ways about it.

By being active, self-disciplined and putting in the hours you will increase the odds for success. The more you do the higher will be the chance that your activities will become a successful result. The less you do the less chances you have to get a lucky punch. Luck is a result of initiating a lot of things and by the law of odds one of them will turn into something big.

Secret 13: You need a motivating vision

If you won't do it, no one else will. No one is doing it for you. If you want something in life you have to do it yourself.

The universe is a great place. Everything is available in abundance. You can have anything that you want.

The first step to getting what you want is to have a thought or a wish in your mind. This thought then needs to be manifested in the real or physical world. You start out with a thought, write it down on paper and then you do the necessary steps to achieve your desired goal.

Walt Disney saw everything first in his mind before he created Disneyland in the real world. We had a clear vision of what he wanted to create and then made a plan and finally created it in the real world.

You should create a vision of what you would like to accomplish in your life. This vision is obviously something that motivates you and that will give you the greatest feeling of satisfaction and accomplishment. The most important thing when creating a vision is the write it down on paper. Otherwise it is merely a thought that will never exist in the real world. My suggestion is to buy an empty journal and write things in it every day. Gather ideas and put them into this one book. Eventually you will have all the information to make your vision a reality.

Remember: dreaming about a goal is great but if you don't write it down, it will soon be forgotten.

Also, you might have a great dream and visualize all kinds of things in abundance. That is great but again: you need to eventually define the things that you want and make some clear decisions. For example if you say that you want to have a big company with lots of employees, then you should decide today how many employees should be working for you. Otherwise it is a fuzzy vision and it will never be put into reality. You need to get absolutely clear in every detail what it is that you want and decide on everything. Only then will you be able to do something about it.

Secret 14: The power of your own power

Most people lack money and they think that the only way to achieve a goal is to have money first. You don't need money to succeed. You have a lot of other assets that you might totally underestimate. You have time, skill, energy, knowledge, contacts and talent.

If you have a clear idea of what you want to achieve you will find that the money will come your way sooner or later. If the idea is good, the money will follow.

You also don't need success gurus or teachers. You have everything inside of you and you need to unlock this power inside of yourself. Most success teachers will motivate you and encourage you to dream big. That is great but no one really tells you how to achieve your goals. Success teachers don't teach you to make baby steps first and focus on simply daily tasks. But that is what you need to do.

There is no secret to success. There is no secret formula or club. You need to simply set a goal, make a plan by breaking it down into little steps and then go to work.

All the power you need already lies within you, not in outside circumstances. Don't give away your power to circumstances like luck, magic tools or other people. Everything you need to know and have is already inside of you.

Too often we give our power away to circumstances: we imagine that we will be more powerful if we would have access to some external tools. We think we'd be happier with more money. We think we could solve all our problems with some magic touch or a lucky strike. And, while waiting for these external circumstances to manifest, we ignore the only real source of power: ourselves.

All you need is to do is trust that you have the power, and then you will succeed.

Secret 15: Keep learning and improving yourself

In order to achieve anything worthwhile, you need to become very good at what you do. You need to constantly improve your skills and make a decision to become the best in your field. You should learn everything there is to learn about your field. You should become a specialist.

You should read all the necessary books on your topic, listen to tapes and go to seminars. Develop the habit of reading at least 30 minutes every day and don't listen to music while you are driving your car. Listen to CDs of successful motivational speakers. Feed your brain with positive input rather than with useless information. By listening to positive messages, your whole personality and outlook will also become more positive.

Secret 16: No one is really better than you and no one is smarter than you

No one is really better than you and no one is smarter than you. Don't ever get intimidated. If other people have achieved great success in one area, then you can do it, too. The only difference between you and a star is simply that this person has figured out how to do it and developed an unshakable desire to achieve it. What someone else has done before you, you can do as well.

Most people have a feeling of inferiority because they don't have a degree or never went to University. Don't let that hold you back psychologically. A lot of successful people never got the diplomas and learned things later in life.

Secret 17: Money raising (selling shares) always comes first

Whatever business idea you might have, in the end it all comes down to selling a product or service to a customer. The more sales you make the higher your profits will be.

Your main focus should be on how to generate more sales or customers. Therefore you should become an expert in sales and marketing.

Your company is not a software company, for example. Your company is a sales generating marketing company. Without sales, there is no company.

This is especially true for Private Equity. If you can't convince investors and financial institutions, you won't be able to raise capital and therefore won't be able to run a successful company. Without money, you can't develop your projects.

Secret 18: The law of concentration

Some people try to be successful with several projects and hope that one of those projects will eventually have a breakthrough. In reality this is not how success works. In order to have a big breakthrough you need to focus your energy on one project or one goal alone.

Let's assume that you have five projects and you can devote 20% of your energy and time to each project. In business there will always be unexpected problems. Usually things take longer than originally thought and cost more than expected. Now if you hope that one of those five projects has a chance then you should think twice. Wouldn't it make more sense to focus full-heartedly with 100% of your time and energy on one project first and make it successful? Your chance of success will be much higher.

To focus on a single project is like a magnifying glass. When the sun shines on to it, there will be much more energy in one place. Average people often get much further in life than geniuses because they don't distract themselves with several things and focus solely on one project.

Secret 19: Remove negative people from your life

Analyze what is holding you back. Sometimes, even if you dream big and are willing to do what is necessary, you might not get ahead.

In that case you need to ask yourself a few questions and analyze what is holding you back.

1. Which is most likely the main factor that slows me down?
2. What could I do to remove this factor?
3. Which person or people are draining emotional energy from me?

Each one of us has certain strengths and weaknesses. No one can be good at everything. This is something that you have to realize. If you are great at presenting your company but weak in doing administrational work and accounting, then you should get or hire professional help for your areas of weakness.

One of the biggest problems why talented people don't get ahead is other people that are holding them back. Sometimes people are in an unhealthy relationship or have people around them that control their lives in a negative way.

You need to remove the negative people in your life. This can be a big step for some but it is necessary to get ahead. You might have to move out of town or leave people behind even if it creates a conflict or fight. But you need to do what is best for yourself and free yourself from people who steal your energy. You need to cut the cord of those energy vampires that suck the life out of you. You need to distance yourself from people who want you to stay where you are and continue to be small. Those people steal your motivation, drive and kill your momentum.

Some people don't even realize that they hold others back. You need to confront them and be very clear about what you want. Most people don't want you to succeed. They want you to be at the same level or below them because of their own inferiority.

This is your life and no one has control over you. You need to do what you feel on the inside is right for you. Only you can make yourself happy.

Secret 20: Change your daily habits and move away from an ordinary life

My advice is to be successful is to follow your heart and create a business in a field that makes you happy.

You might ask the question: "What if everybody does that? Where would we end up? Somebody has to do the regular work."

The good thing is that this will never be the case and because of that you have a good chance of realizing your dreams. Distance yourself from the ordinary life and take a look at it. If you continue to do what the masses are doing, nothing will change for the better. Most people go to work from 9 to 5, pay bills and worry about money. Is this really what you want to be?

You first need to realize this and then do something different. You need to rethink your life and your habits. What is holding you back? Who or what is stealing your time? Which people should you no longer associate yourself with?

Assuming you get up every morning at seven. You take a shower, read the newspaper, watch the morning news, eat breakfast and talk to your neighbor about the weather and then you get to work. Seems like a typical morning for a working person, doesn't it?

You could on the other hand get up at 5:00 am because you went to bed earlier the night before and did not watch TV. Then you go running for thirty minutes, develop your plans and goals, read something that will get you ahead in your field and work a half an hour on a new business project that will allow you to quit your current job in the near future. Then you eat breakfast and go to work.

By comparing these two examples what comes to mind? What if you not only changed those two hours in the morning but also the rest of your day? How about your lunch break? What about the weekends? What if you got rid of your TV?

You need to be aware of your daily habits and change those that are not useful. Did you hear the expression that there is a price for success that needs to be paid? Well, this is it. Changing your daily habits. Giving up certain things. Being more self-disciplined. That is the real price of success.

Secret 21: Success is not difficult—it's all in your mind

Success is easy. Success is easy in America and in Europe. In Bangladesh or Cambodia success is hard. Think about all the possibilities and options there are. If you don't believe that then you will be struggling your whole life. In the first world countries the money basically lies in the streets. You just have to do something and pick it up.

There are all kinds of options for you to make money in this world. We live in the richest and best time ever. Never before has it been easier to create wealth. Technology has made it possible for everyone with little or no money to create a business that can grow internationally. The Internet has opened up options that have never been there before.

Which false beliefs do you still have that keep you from a life that you deserve?

There is so much money and possibilities in this world. It would be crazy not to get a piece of the pie. What are you waiting for?

Secret 22: Everything is a numbers game

Selling a product or service has a lot to do with the law of probability. Whatever it is that you sell, there are always a certain percentage of people who will buy your product. So the more people you talk to, the more sales you will make. You can literally calculate how much money you want to make. Selling is like math. There is always a percentage.

Try to think in numbers when it comes to your business. You need to be able to calculate the numbers of efforts that need to be done in order to achieve an end result.

You might have to talk to 1000 people first before you can make a sale. But in the end there is always somebody who will buy your product. The question is only which sales channels work better and what you can do to improve the individual steps in your sales process to get better numbers. The more people come into contact with your product or service, the more sales you will have in the end. This is the law of probability.

It is only a matter of the amount of acquisition efforts that you have to do in order to be successful. The only person standing in your way might be yourself. If you are not lazy or afraid of rejection, there is no limit to what you can achieve.

Secret 23: Clear written goals

The number one reason why people don't get in life what they want is because they don't know what it is exactly what they want.

80% of your success will depend on clarity. People who plan are four times more successful than people who don't plan. The absence of clarity is the biggest factor of frustration and failure than any other factor.

Most people never write a business plan. A business plan is time consuming and hard work. Most people believe that they have all their ideas in their head and that there is no need for a business plan.

If you are one of those people, I need to warn you. You might lose a lot of money and time if you fail to write a business plan.

The process of writing a business plan is so crucial because it forces you to think your idea all the way through and get complete clarity. There might be something in your business process that you have not considered before but it turns out to be a hugely important step if you want to make it work.

The more clarity you will have for yourself, the faster you will move forward. If you are very clear about your plans, you are going to be a better sales person and presenter because you will come across with confidence.

Secret 24: Marketing and sales is key

74% of all self-made millionaires are directly involved in sales. 74%! That is almost everybody! That is why it is so important that you learn everything about selling.
Remember that buying and selling is the very foundation of each business transaction.

No matter what your business does, your company is a marketing company. You can have the best products in the world but if you don't sell anything, you won't have a company for long.

Your main focus must be on getting new clients and generating sales. You can only achieve this if you make marketing and sales your number one priority. Your product doesn't matter, your philosophy is irrelevant, your product design is pointless if you don't make marketing and sales the number one topic.

You need to become a master at marketing and sales. Actually, every one of us is already an expert. You are being bombarded daily with offers and people who try to sell something to you. Instinctively, you know what works and what doesn't. Often, common sense is a better judge than any fancy strategy that someone tries to teach you.

You need three things to be able to sell something:

1. A product or service
2. A sales message
3. A sales channel

Most people focus too much on the product. Much more important is the message and how you are selling the product.

Secret 25: Your energy will get others to follow you—not money

In the financial world only money or things that can be turned into money are viewed as assets. Assets are a lot more, however. Assets are all the things that you can bring to the table. If you don't have money it is not the end of the world. You have other things: creativity, willingness to work and time! Those things are also assets.

Your attitude and power to make things happen are the biggest assets that you have—not money!

You will create wealth out of your creativity and your thoughts. You need the willingness to do whatever is necessary and to believe in yourself. You have all you need in excess!
Our biggest obstacle is not the scarcity of money. It is the scarcity of all the other factors! If your ideas are good the money will flow where it is needed.

Secret 26: Become a specialist

Become a specialist in your field. Learn everything there is to know about your field. No one can be good at everything.
But once you have chosen a specific field or industry for yourself, you should make a commitment to become absolutely the best in your field.

Read all the important books, take all the courses, speak to the best people in your field, read all the news and inform yourself in any way you can.

The better you are at what you do the more business you will get. People like to deal with absolutely the best. If you develop a reputation to be the best at what you do then you will be amazed what will happen.

Who would you rather perform your brain surgery: A brain surgeon who does two operations per day or a general medical doctor?

Secret 27: Decide to become the best

The next statement seems so obvious that most will easily dismiss it as: "well that is clear!" And here it goes:

> If you want to get to the top, you need to
> make a decision to get to the top.

Most people don't realize how important this is. If you make a real decision, it is almost as if you swear to do it. You could even go as far as saying that you will not rest until it is accomplished even if it is the last thing on earth that you will do.

Making a real decision comes with consequences. If you decide to do something, you make the decision to do it whole-heartedly or not at all. If you think that your goal is "nice to have" but not really a must when it comes down to it, then it is not a real decision.

You need to think about all the possible consequences for your life and be aware what it really means. If you still want it, then you need to make a pact with yourself and close all other options. This decision needs to be so strong that you are ready to give your whole life for it. There cannot be a plan B.

You know that doing something with a limited motivation just won't do anymore. You can't be a sailboat without a sail. You can't be lost in the masses and having an average result. If you decide to do something, you need to decide to go all the way to the top—nothing less.

So think very clearly about what it is that you want and then make a real decision and never look back.

Secret 28: Everything happens for a reason

Become all you can be. The law of cause and effect says that everything happens for a reason. If you want to be successful, you need to think thoughts of success first. You need to do the things first, before you can enjoy success.

The law of cause of effect is a law of nature or a so-called universal law. It is one of the things that you cannot change, avoid or ignore. It is also called the law of action and reaction. It states that everything that happens had a preceding action before it occurred.

> Everything in our world is based on the
> laws of nature or universal laws.
> Everything happens of a reason.

The world is still full of people who are not happy with their results but do the same things and expect a different result. If you want something to change in your life, you need to do things differently than you did before.

> Most people achieve far less than they are capable of achieving.

The law of cause and effect does not only apply to your actions alone. Every action is always preceded by a thought in your mind. In order to change things, you need to change your thoughts or your thinking. This is the initial cause for everything.

If you have positive and encouraging thoughts, it is much more likely that you will achieve a positive result.

The quality of your thoughts is key. Think positive and expect good things to happen.

On the other hand, negative thoughts will prevent you from being successful.

The law of cause and effect is very real. It is like the law of gravity. Even though you can't see it, doesn't mean that it doesn't exist.

Your outer world is a mirror of your inner world. You are who you are because of the thoughts that you have thought. Start thinking like other successful people in your area and you will get the same results. By changing your causes, therefore, your thinking, you will change your results.

Secret 29: The truth will always be the best strategy

The truth will set you free and give you strength and self-confidence.

> Always live in truth with the people around you and your circumstances.

Never live a lie. It takes away energy and pride from you. Never stay in a situation that makes you unhappy or that is wrong for you. Never disillusion yourself about the truth. If it doesn't feel right, you should get out. Your inner peace and contentment should be your highest priority. Nothing will take away more power and self-confidence if you live a life where you have to hide the truth. Being able to communicate the truth in every situation is liberating and empowering even if it is temporarily to your disadvantage.

There are three things in life that cannot stay hidden for long: The sun, the moon and the truth.

Secret 30: Develop your communication and sales skills

In order to be successful in life general—not just in business— you need to be able to deal with people. The better you can communicate and influence people the more successful you will become.

In whatever you do, you always need to sell yourself. You sell your person to your clients, your boss, your point of view, etc.

The one book that changed the way I communicated with people is Dale Carnegie's classic "How To Win Friends and Influence People". It has helped me to develop better communication skills and improve the quality of how I interact with people. I strongly recommend that you read this book. It will change your life.

The most important lesson I learned was about criticism and praise. Nothing can destroy a relationship faster than insulting a person or criticizing that person in front of others.

Selling is really nothing else but being a really good communicator and understanding the behavior of people and knowing what motivates them. If you can help others get what they want, you can get what you want. Therefore I strongly suggest that you learn everything about selling. Becoming a better communicator will give you tremendous self-confidence because you know you can deal with every person—especially the difficult ones.

Secret 31: Always dress like a successful businessperson

Your self-image is also an important factor. Have you ever tried to make phone calls to clients in your pajamas at home? It is not the same feeling as if you were dressed up in a suit and tie and call clients from the office. You feel better about yourself and you feel more business-like. You have more self-confidence and you wear clothes that reflect your business attitude.

Justified or not—people judge you all the time. Especially in the first 30 seconds of meeting someone new, people make their judgment. As a person who wants to get ahead in life, it is important to dress accordingly. You will get more respect and you are not "hurting" yourself by being overdressed.

Secret 32: Get into shape and have a healthy lifestyle

In order to have a high level of self-confidence and more energy you need to feel good about yourself. When you look in the mirror and you feel like you have gained too much weight over the years and you remember how you used to look, you might not feel great about yourself. It is important that you get into good shape.

You should work out each day for at least thirty minutes and improve your level of fitness. It will not only improve your body and energy level but mainly it will give you a mental improvement that you might underestimate today. You will feel better about yourself and with more energy and more mental power you will be able to conquer bigger goals and tasks.

You will only reach your full potential if you are healthy and energetic. Free yourself from bad nutrition, alcohol, drugs, smoking and other unhealthy habits. Your mind will only function well if it is in a healthy body.

Secret 33: Think positive thoughts and expect only the best

Free yourself from limiting beliefs. You can be, do or have anything in this life. You have more talent and abilities than you can imagine. You can learn anything about any topic there is. There is nothing that you cannot do. If someone else has already done or achieved something that you want, you can achieve it, too. You need to do the same things that this person did. You need to learn exactly what they knew and then copy it. You came into this world as a human being with a super brain that gives you unlimited possibilities. You need to be aware of your own power. People, life and past experiences have undermined your real strength. Now is the time to let it all go and come back to your powerful roots of who you really are and what you can do.

Secret 34: Free yourself from negative people and circumstances

Free yourself from the approval from others. Stop worrying about what other people might think when you are trying to achieve your goals. Other people can be an emotional block and refrain you from putting your energy full-heartedly into any undertaking. It is a normal part of life that not everybody will approve of what you are doing. There is always a negative or jealous person that doesn't want you to succeed. You need to be aware of that and purposely distance yourself and your thoughts from people who don't want you to succeed. Ask yourself: Who are they to tell you what you should or shouldn't do? No one can tell you what to do. No one is better than you.

Secret 35: Make a decision to never give up

Once you have decided on a specific goal you should make the conscious decision to never give up. This decision will empower you and give you more self-confidence than anything else. Even if things go really bad, you will continue to give everything you have.

Nothing can stop you. Basically, it is very simple. All you need is a goal, a plan, self-discipline, time and the conviction that you will never quit.

> There are people in this world that had ten times more obstacles in their way than you do now. So don't find excuses.

I want to share a conversation between a young entrepreneur and a millionaire with you. The entrepreneur was just about to give up before he had this talk.

Millionaire: "Ok, you have no more money. But do you still believe in your idea?"
Entrepreneur: "Yes."

Millionaire: "Do you still have regular meals?"
Entrepreneur: "Yes."

Millionaire: "Do you have a place to sleep even if it is someone's couch or inside of your car?"
Entrepreneur: "Yes."

Millionaire: "Do you have people in your life that love and support you even though they think you are a little bit crazy?"

Entrepreneur: "Yes."

Millionaire: "Then you should continue. You will make it sooner or later!"

We live in a society that is rich in so many ways. We often tend to forget that fact. You can go to any supermarket and buy a piece of meat. You don't have to go out and hunt it yourself. You can go to a public library and get all the knowledge in the world for free. You have social services that will help you if you are at the bottom.

Don't give up too easily if things don't work out your way. What can really happen to you? You can lose all your money. So what? You don't die because of this. You can always get a job again. But isn't it worth the risk to live your dream and have a chance of becoming financially independent?

Life is sometimes like a game. You can play it safe and stay in a job for the rest of your life. Or you can try to win the game of life? If things don't work out, change something. If it still doesn't work out, change something else. Sooner or later your success is guaranteed because you will have figured it out.

Secret 36: You must be able to deal with rejection and temporary setbacks

> If you have a setback it is a true test to see if you really want it.

Temporary setbacks are an inevitable part of life. You cannot become better or stronger if you don't fail or have a setback from time to time. The most important thing is to learn from your mistakes and not beating yourself up over it.

Especially when you are in sales or business you will be confronted with rejection. Don't ever take rejection personally. The more rejection you get, the better you will be able to deal with it.

I often compare it with having baby skin in the beginning. Baby skin is soft and you can easily hurt it. Eventually, your baby skin will turn into elephant skin and nothing can hurt you anymore.

The key is to stay positive.

If you are spiritual you could look at it this way: God is not interested in making our lives easy. He is much more interested in building our character. God's delay is not God's rejection.

But here is a really interesting way of looking at it: Let's say that you want a bigger house. You set it as a goal and you dream about it. But then one day something happens. Your existing house burns down. At first, we all have the tendency to think: why did this happen to me? Why do I have such bad luck? But in reality, the Universe wanted to give you a bigger house and it needed to get rid of the old house first so that the new one could come into your life. Things that appear negative at first can actually turn out to be a positive event. But it is important to try to see the positive things in every situation.

Final words of encouragement

> We all must suffer from one of two things:
> Either the pain of self-discipline or the pain
> of regret and disappointment.
> (Jim Rohn)

Never be lazy. The price that you are paying for being lazy or being scared is regret, disappointment and frustration. There is no need to save your energy for anything right now. Go out with courage and conquer the world with everything that you have got. The reward will be ten times of what you could hope for. You just have to trust the Universe and in all that is possible in this world.

Go out there and make it happen. I want to thank you for reading my book. I hope that you understand the power of the information that I have given and that you can improve your life and the lives of others.

About Norman Meier

Norman Meier has been an investment professional since 1995. He has held executive positions with top-tier global investment firms such as MAN Investments and AWD in Switzerland, and Canaccord Capital Corporation in Canada. He also founded a Swiss financial services firm, which has been licensed by the Swiss Banking Commission and registered with a self-regulatory organization.

Norman Meier is highly educated. He has a BBA, MBA and Ph D in Human Behavior from Newport University. His MBA has a concentration in "Interpersonal Relationship & Communication" and his Ph D is concentrated in "Personnel Management".

He had originally received the Swiss Matura Type D (languages) and went to the University of Zurich to study Psychology. After his service in the army, he received a Financial Planning Designation of AWD Switzerland where he worked for over six years. He continued to journey to Canada where he finished several courses and received designations in from the Canadian Securities Institute (equivalent to FINRA in the USA):

- Canadian Securities Course (CSC)—Diploma
- Derivatives Fundamental Course (DFC)—Diploma
- Conduct & Practices Handbook Course (CPH)—Diploma
- Options Licensing Course (OLC)—Diploma
- Ethics Case Study Course
- Technical Analysis Course (TAC)—Diploma
- Investment Management Techniques (IMT)—Diploma
- Options Strategies Course (OSTC)—Diploma
- Portfolio Management Techniques (PMT)—Diploma
- Agricultural Markets—Risk Management (ARM)—Diploma

- FCSI—Fellowship of the Canadian Securities Institute Designation (Highest honor in the financial services industry in Canada)
- Canadian Investment Manager Designation
- Derivatives Market Specialist Designation

He got a license from the Swiss Banking Commission (EBK—Eidgenoessische Bankenkommission) to sell investment products (like mututal funds, etc.) and was member of the largest Swiss self-regulatory organization (SRO): VQF—Verein für Qualitätssicherung von Finanzdienstleistungen. Later he also became a member with his company Sedona AG with Polyreg, another Swiss self-regulatory organization against money laundering.

In 2011 he became licensed with FINRA in the US and got his Series 7 and Series 63 license, which made him officially licensed to sell securities in the US. He has an absolute clean record.

Norman Meier was the manager of a FINRA licensed broker dealer in USA and CEO and president of a two public mining exploration companies. He was the founder and major shareholder of several gold and uranium exploration companies in the US and major shareholder of three sales organizations in Europe.

He built up a global team of over 60 employees in Switzerland, USA, Canada and Mexico. He was the president and founder of a Swiss financial services company with a license from a self-regulatory organization and a license from the Swiss Banking Commission.

He has built up client base of over 3000 clients worldwide, he has 15 finance diplomas and designations; he has raised over $400 million for all kinds of financial products from private clients and $600 million from institutional clients. He has been licensed in Switzerland, Canada and the US to sell securities and his record is absolutely clean and perfect.

Norman Meier has over 10 years of experience in the gold exploration and production industry. He has become a real specialist who not only understands the financial and business side of a public company but as well as the actual technical knowledge and processes in the gold industry. He (or though the companies that he worked for) held over 25 different projects all over the world. Most of these projects were gold, silver, copper and molybdenum. Norman Meier took two gold companies public in USA and Germany, managed over 10 geologists and owned projects in Canada, USA, Mexico and Peru.

Having attended a lot of seminars himself at a very young age, Norman Meier received training about success and psychology during his childhood. His father Prof. Dr. Eddie Meier is a professor in psychology and gave seminars and taught courses all his life. Norman Meier was able to benefit from his father's experience and personally came across and met other successful teachers like Anthony Robbins, Brian Tracy, Vera Birkenbihl, Bodo Schaefer just to name a few.

Norman Meier started teaching sales techniques, communication, financial planning, real estate financing and mutual fund basics to large groups of people. He also has given sales seminars to various companies and usually presented seminars in front more than 50 people at a time.

Norman Meier has published six books to date including this one. Four of those books are in German and two are in English. His first book is called "Vorher—nachher" (before and after) and is a fitness book. He wrote this book over ten years ago because he competed in two bodybuilding competitions himself.

His second book is called "Den eigenen Traum leben" (live your own dream) and is about finding your own way in life.

His third book is called "Der Traum vom eigenen Business (the dream of your own business) and is about turning an idea into a business.

His fourth book is called "Verkaufspsychologie" (Sales psychology) and teaches sales people the basics about selling and psychology including sales techniques and methods.

And his latest book is called "Start your own business and live your dream" is his first English book and talks about how to start your own business.

Norman Meier has two times Swiss Aerobics champion and competed in the World championships in Tokyo in 1995. He has a third degree black belt in karate and won many tournaments from 1990 to 1999. He also competed in two bodybuilding competitions in 2005 and 2006 in Europe. He was also first runner up in the Mr. Switzerland competition 1994.

Norman Meier grew up in Switzerland and speaks five languages. His first language is Swiss German. He is happily married and has four children. He furthermore has a love for animals in need and supports several charities